Paleo
Slow Cooking

Paleo
Slow Cooking

*Over 140 Practical, Primal, Whole-Food
Recipes for the Electric Slow Cooker*

Dominique DeVito

with Breea Johnson, M.S., R.D., L.D.N.

CIDER MILL PRESS

BOOK PUBLISHERS

Kennebunkport, Maine

13-Digit ISBN: 978-1-60433-336-7
10-Digit ISBN: 1-60433-336-7

This book may be ordered by mail from the publisher. Please include $5.95 for postage and handling.
Please support your local bookseller first!

Books published by Cider Mill Press Book Publishers are available at special discounts for bulk purchases in the United States by corporations, institutions, and other organizations. For more information, please contact the publisher.

Cider Mill Press Book Publishers
"Where good books are ready for press"
12 Spring Street
PO Box 454
Kennebunkport, Maine 04046

Visit us on the Web!
www.cidermillpress.com

Design by Alicia Freile, Tango Media
Typeset by Gwen Galeone, Tango Media
Typography: Archer, Chaparral Pro, Helvetica Neue and Voluta
All images used under license from Shutterstock.com.
Printed in China

3 4 5 6 7 8 9 10

Contents

What Is the Paleo Diet, and Why Is It Good for Me?

*F*irst, congratulations on your interest in the Paleo diet. You'll soon learn that going Paleo is about more than just diet, though it certainly starts there. It's also about making choices for a healthier lifestyle all around. And that's wonderful.

Like any bold change you want to make to better your health, however, this one will require some sacrifices and will take some getting used to. This may sound discouraging, but it's important to be honest. The Paleo plan requires that you give up foods that you may have learned to associate with comfort and good times, like sugar, white bread and potatoes, processed foods, and dairy. I know, it sounds scary. The good news—and it's really good news!—is that the sacrifices you'll make have huge payoffs for your health.

Within the first few weeks of making the change to the Paleo diet, you should experience:

* Increased energy
* Moderate weight loss
* Improved digestion
* Improved skin tone and hair condition
* Improved mood, including more restful sleep

If these are the benefits you're seeking, you won't be disappointed. The added bonus of this book is that you'll learn to use the slow cooker to keep you on the Paleo diet. This means that you'll have a collection of recipes that will make eating—and enjoying meals—easy and affordable at the same time you'll be reaping the benefits of Paleo.

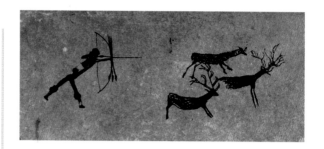

What Is Paleo?

"Paleo" is short for Paleolithic. This was the time period dating from approximately 2 million to 12,000 BCE. Next was the Mesolithic Era, from roughly 12,000 to 8,000 BCE, and the Neolithic Era, or roughly 8,000 to 5,000 BCE and the transition to a more agricultural, domestic lifestyle for ancient humans. The Paleolithic era is also referred to as the Stone Age. It is when our ancestors became much more skilled at hunting with stone tools, which enabled them to hunt animals more effectively. For most of this period, humans were simple hunter-gatherers, competing for food sources with the likes of wooly mammoths and savage wooly rhinoceroses, giant deer, bison, musk ox, and hare. They were much more in synch with their environments—out of necessity—and adapted to the demands of the day, spending many hours foraging and hunting.

Because caves afforded some of the best protection against the wildlife and the elements, we have come to refer to our ancestors of these eras as "cavemen," and thus the Paleo(lithic) diet is sometimes referred to as the caveman diet. It is a simplification, of course, but it also provides a great concept for the diet, which is one based largely on meat, fish, eggs, vegetables, and fruits. It's also a fitting concept for the lifestyle of Paleo people—active, ever watchful, keenly aware of their surroundings.

Paleo for the Modern World

Though we may be borrowing from the concept of "necessity" eating and activity from our Paleo brethren (and sistren), be glad we are living in today's modern world where, for us, this is a choice rather than a necessity. If we had to get out there and bring down our meals on a regular basis, we wouldn't have time to read—or write—cookbooks such as these! We've come a long way, baby—for real!—and there's no need to go backward. That's another great thing about today's Paleo diet (and this cookbook): It contains far more variety than a caveperson could have ever conceived of, and healthier means of preparation, as well!

Another consideration for the modern Paleo is the very real awareness of the impact of domesticated meat production on the planet. Cavemen weren't killing herds of black Angus beef cattle; they were taking on animals in the wild. And the caveman population wasn't at nearly 7 billion worldwide. If everyone went Paleo, the increased demand for domesticated meat could do more harm than good on a global level.

These are discussion points beyond the scope of this cookbook but ones that Paleo enthusiasts debate frequently, and rightly so. As the benefits of the diet to their overall health make them even greater supporters of it, they explore more and more of its aspects. One of the founding fathers of the Paleo diet and lifestyle is Loren Cordain, PhD. He is the author of *The Paleo Diet* and several spinoffs from that book. He speaks about the diet around the world. He has a website (www.the paleodiet.com) and a blog and is considered "the leading expert on paleolithic diets and founder of the paleo movement." He is an excellent resource to tap into as you learn more about Paleo.

And now, let's eat!

Chapter 1

The Paleo Pantry

*T*his is the part of going Paleo where the rubber meets the road, where your commitment will come smack up against your current eating habits. It's not that you won't be able to fill your pantry and fridge with a great selection of Paleo-friendly foods. It's just that in order to do that, you first need to eliminate the foods that aren't part of the Paleo diet.

Out Before In

Get started by finding a sturdy cardboard box or some of your larger recyclable grocery bags, as you want to be able to pack up the intact packages of foods you won't be needing anymore and easily take them to a family member, friend, or your local food pantry.

Start with your pantry. You want to remove any grains—rice of any kind, pasta, noodles, quinoa, oatmeal, and so forth.

You'll also want to purge your shelves of any foods that include sugar. Read the labels if you're uncertain, as this includes any artificial sweeteners, as well, and there are many of them. Some of the more common are saccharine, aspartame, sucralose, corn syrup, and high fructose corn syrup.

Next, remove any containers of processed oils—vegetable oil, canola oil, and peanut oil are some of the more popular. Anything that is hydrogenated or partially hydrogenated has to go. Don't worry; fats are a necessary part of a Paleo diet and good health, and there are several on the "must-have" list.

While vegetables are a major component of the Paleo diet, legumes are off limits, as they contain anti-nutrients and contribute to digestive distress and bloating. Legumes include most types of beans, including kidney, garbanzo, pinto, fava, and soy. You may be surprised how many legumes you have in your pantry, as they are staples in soups, stews, and even salads. Fortunately, legumes that are more pod than pea can be included in the diet (more on those later).

Move on to your refrigerator and freezer. Say goodbye to dairy—milk, butter or margarine, cheese, yogurt, ice cream. Say goodbye to bottled salad dressings, deli meats, juices, and anything that contains nitrates, sweeteners, artificial ingredients, or other non-Paleo ingredients, as mentioned above.

To summarize, here's what you want to get out of your kitchen:
* Pastas and other grains
* Oatmeal
* Breakfast cereals
* Granola
* Rice
* Breads, crackers, chips
* Sugar, including brown, light brown, and confectioner's
* Artificial sweeteners and products that contain them
* Candy and cookies
* Vegetable oil
* Canola oil
* Peanut oil
* Sunflower oil
* Corn oil
* Soybean oil
* Shortening

* Peanut butter, mixed nuts (especially cocktail peanuts)
* Cans or bags of beans—red, kidney, pinto, lima, garbanzo
* Jams and jellies
* Salad dressings
* Soy sauce
* Packaged sauces or condiments, including ketchup and mustard
* Milk, butter, cream, margarine, yogurt, ice cream, and other dairy

Now heed this advice: Take away the foods you've removed immediately! You do not want to be tempted by any of them!

In and Begin

Once you've removed the no-no's, it's time to stock up on what will become the staples of your new, healthier diet. Besides referencing the lists here, browse through this cookbook and take note of ingredients that sound especially good. Remember, one of the main reasons that a Paleo diet can be so healthy for you is that it is focused on fresher, more easily digested food sources. When considering what to stock up on, always think fresh.

Be forewarned: Your body will go through cravings for foods you once took for granted—especially those with sugar—and you'll want to be sure you have the makings of something really tasty so you can feel good about your decision and stick with your commitment.

For the Cupboard

Most of your ancillary ingredients on the Paleo diet will be seasonings, as the essentials are truly simple: meat, fish, eggs, vegetables, fruits, and berries. Depending on how old some of your current seasonings are, you may want to start over. Stock up on seasonings so you have lots of options when it's time to cook. And while it's important to have a great selection of seasonings, remember that fresher is always better, so use fresh herbs when you can.

Stock up on:
* Dried herbs, including parsley, oregano, chives, mint, basil, thyme, tarragon, sage, bay leaves, and rosemary
* Ground spices, including cayenne pepper, cumin, coriander, ginger, nutmeg, clove, curry powder, allspice, paprika, chili powder, mustard, and cardamom
* Pepper and iodized sea salt

There are all kinds of spice combinations on the market today, and almost all are fair game for Paleo cooking. Just be sure to read the ingredients and make sure they don't contain artificial sweeteners or preservatives.

Oils and Other Staples

Your pantry will look woefully bare without cans and jars and containers of beans, jams, cereals, pasta, spaghetti sauces, and snacks. Yikes! Time to move in what's Paleo-approved:

* Oils contribute necessary fats to a diet and are essential for cooking. Those that can be used for a Paleo diet are extra-virgin olive oil, coconut oil (unrefined), avocado oil, nut oils (like walnut or almond), and seed oils (flax and sesame, for example).
* Dried fruits, which make for great snacks— in moderation and with no additional sweetener added.
* Dry or roasted nuts, like almonds, walnuts, pistachios, and cashews. Again, in moderation.
* Broths and stocks, including chicken, beef and vegetable broths, so long as there are no sugars or soy in them.

* Vinegars, including apple cider and coconut.
* Olives packed in water with minimal salt.
* Pickles jarred without sugars or chemicals.
* Canned fish packed in water or olive oil (not soybean oil), including tuna, salmon, and sardines.
* Tomato paste and salsa without added sugar, corn, or wheat.
* Fish sauce.
* Coconut aminos (a soy-free seasoning sauce that's loaded with amino acids).

Protein Sources

Proteins comprise the bulk of the Paleo diet, so it's important to shop smart for what is healthiest. For meats like beef, lamb, and pork, you want to be sure you're purchasing grass-fed, organically raised sources. Poultry should be free-range. The best fish is wild-caught, and cold-water, oily fishes like herring, anchovies, mackerel, salmon, and sardines are the highest in Omega-3 fatty acids.

The most economical way to stock up on meats and fish is to buy in bulk if possible. Find a farmer at a farmer's market whose meats meet with your approval, and talk to him or her about purchasing a side of an animal. It may be worth investing in a freezer to accommodate this quantity, but it is definitely more economical in the long run.

The Paleo diet includes high-quality sources of:
* Beef
* Pork
* Lamb
* Poultry
* Eggs
* Fish and seafood
* Game meats (pheasant, boar, bear, elk, etc.)

Remember, too, that organ meats (liver, kidneys, brain) were a true Paleo staple (and often the highest-prized cuts), so be sure to keep these in your freezer. Slow cooking is a great way to mellow out some of the pungency in these cuts, making them as tender and flavorful as traditional cuts.

Vegetables

There are three words to describe stocking up on this part of the Paleo diet: Go for it!

The only items you'll need to avoid in the produce section of your grocery store—or at the farmer's market—are corn and white potatoes. So whether your tastes run to leafy greens, crunchy carrots, zucchini, squashes, cabbage and Brussels sprouts, asparagus, beets, even artichokes—indulge in them and enjoy.

Fruits and Berries

As you transition to Paleo, if you've been used to ending your meals with a sweet treat, the sugar monster will haunt you. It will seem like everywhere you look there are sweet foods that you can't eat, from a decadent fruit-topped cheesecake to an itty-bitty dark chocolate chip.

To help beat back the sugar monster, be sure you have fruits and berries with you at all times. Keep a small bag of dried fruit in the car or in your desk drawer, and treat them like the dark chocolate chip you would allow yourself at mid-day. If you crave something soft and sweet, turn to a ripe banana, which you can get almost any time of year.

Like the abundance of availability of vegetables, the same can be said of fruits and berries. You can enjoy oranges, apples, tangerines, strawberries, raspberries, peaches, pineapples, grapes, melons—even watermelon.

Sauces and Dressings

There's no need to go without ketchup, barbecue sauce, mayonnaise, tartar sauce, or satay sauce just because store-bought varieties aren't Paleo. These sauces and dressings aren't made in the slow cooker, but they're helpful to know how to prepare so you can make your Paleo meals even tastier.

Paleomayo

Mayonnaise is essentially eggs and oil, which are both Paleo-friendly! It's the emulsification process that turns these ingredients into the thick, delicious sauce we call mayo. This recipe will have you hooked on homemade.

2 egg yolks
½ teaspoon dry mustard
3 teaspoons freshly squeezed lemon juice
½ cup olive oil
½ cup coconut oil, melted and at room temperature (not warm)
Salt and pepper to taste

1. In a food processor, add yolks, mustard, and 1 teaspoon of lemon juice. Pulse to combine.

2. With the processor on, slowly (and I mean *slowly*— in a drizzle!) add the olive oil, then the melted coconut oil. You'll see the eggs and oil begin to emulsify as you continue to slowly add the oil. When all oil is in, transfer the mayo to a bowl using a spatula to scrape it out of the food processor.

3. Fold in the remaining 2 teaspoons of lemon juice, and season with salt and pepper. Store in an airtight container in the refrigerator for up to 7 to 10 days.

Paleo BBQ Sauce

This concoction is tangy, smoky, and smooth. Play around with the quantities of seasonings until you discover the proportions that taste best for you.

2 cups Caveman ketchup
½ cup coconut crystals
1 tablespoon dry mustard
1 teaspoons cayenne (red pepper)
½ teaspoons allspice
¼ cup liquid smoke (optional)
2 tablespoons fresh-squeezed lemon juice

1. In a saucepan over medium heat, combine all ingredients, stirring well. Cook while stirring constantly. When liquid starts to boil, reduce heat to low. Continue stirring and cooking for another 5 to 7 minutes.

2. Allow to cool before serving. Sauce can be stored in an airtight container in the refrigerator for 7 to 10 days.

Caveman Ketchup

Traditional ketchup has sweetener in it, so it takes a bit of getting used to when you make your own sugar-free version. But it's much cleaner and better for you.

1 15-oz can tomato sauce

1 6-oz can tomato paste

1 tablespoon cider vinegar

¼ teaspoon onion powder

2 cloves garlic, peeled and crushed through a garlic press

¼ teaspoon allspice

Salt and pepper, to taste

1. In a small saucepan, mix tomato sauce, tomato paste, vinegar, onion powder, garlic, and all-spice with a whisk to combine thoroughly.

2. Heat over medium high, whisking gently every once in a while as it heats. Cook for about 10 minutes. Add salt, pepper, and cayenne.

3. Allow to cool, and store in an airtight glass jar in the refrigerator for up to 7 to 10 days.

Variation:
❋ For some extra zing, add a pinch of cayenne pepper.

Tartar Sauce

Since fish is one of the staples of a Paleo diet, you'll want to have some homemade tartar sauce.

¾ cup Paleo mayo

¼ cup butter pickles, finely chopped

1 tablespoon fresh parsley, finely chopped

2 teaspoons coconut milk

2 teaspoons white wine vinegar

½ teaspoon red onion, finely diced

½ teaspoon dry mustard

In a small bowl, combine all ingredients. Stir well until thoroughly blended. Store in an airtight glass container in the refrigerator, where it will keep up to 2 weeks.

Nut Butter Satay

Satay is a Thai dipping sauce for grilled meats that is usually made with peanuts or peanut butter. This recipe uses almond butter. You could also use cashew or walnut butter.

½ cup almond butter
½ cup water
2 teaspoons sesame oil
4 tablespoons rice vinegar
2 teaspoons fresh-squeezed lime juice
½ teaspoon Asian red chili sauce

Combine all ingredients in a bowl and stir to combine thoroughly. Store in an airtight container in the refrigerator for up to 7 to 10 days, but serve at room temperature.

Super-Fresh Salsa

The great thing about making your own salsa is that you can skip the sugar, which is found in so many premade versions. Serve this super-fresh salsa with grilled chicken, fish, and veggies for a tasty treat. Ole!

3 large, very ripe tomatoes
½ small red onion, peeled and minced
1 jalapeno pepper, seeded and minced
2 tablespoons fresh cilantro, coarsely chopped
1 lime, squeezed
½ teaspoon salt
¼ teaspoon freshly ground black pepper

Cut tomatoes in half and scoop out all seeds. Coarsely chop the tomatoes and put into a large bowl. Add remainder of ingredients. Stir to combine, and refrigerate to let flavors meld. Store in a tightly sealed glass container for up to 7 days.

Mint Sauce

This is fantastic with lamb, of course, but also pairs nicely with gamier meats like goose or dark meat turkey.

1 bunch fresh mint (a large handful), leaves removed from stems, washed, and dried
1 cup olive oil
2 tablespoons white wine vinegar
1 tablespoon fresh-squeezed lemon juice
1 teaspoon honey
½ teaspoon salt

1. On a cutting board, coarsely chop the mint leaves, and put them in a glass container with a lid, like a Mason jar.

2. In a small bowl, whisk together the oil, vinegar, lemon juice, honey, and salt. Pour over the mint leaves. Secure the lid and shake the mixture vigorously.

3. Refrigerate and let sit until ready to use. It'll keep for about a month.

Paleo Pesto

This is such a great condiment when basil is fresh and in season! Make extra and freeze it in an ice cube tray so you can add it to vegetables or as a topping on meat any time of the year.

½ cup pine nuts (pignoli) or walnuts, toasted
6 cups basil leaves, coarse stems removed, washed and dried thoroughly
4 cloves garlic, chopped
½ cup olive oil
¼ teaspoon salt

1. Place a heavy-bottomed saucepan over medium heat. When hot, add the nuts and stir constantly to warm them from all sides and to keep them from overheating or burning. The idea is to warm and brown them to release aromas and oils. If you burn them, you have to start over. When nuts are toasted, set aside.

2. Make sure the basil leaves are completely dry. If they've been recently washed, let them sit out a bit even after drying them with a towel to ensure they are dry.

3. In a food processor, combine the basil and garlic. Using a pulsing action, slowly pour the olive oil in through the top to combine it with the basil and garlic. Continue to pulse slowly while adding the olive oil in a slow stream. When all the oil is in the processor, pulse on high until pesto is a saucy consistency.

4. Season with salt. Store in an airtight container for 7 to 10 days—or in an ice cube tray, if you want to freeze small portions.

Chapter 2

Slow Going:

A Guide to Slow Cookers and the Wonders of Slow Cooking

*L*uckily for all of us who are "science challenged," it doesn't take a degree in physics to operate a slow cooker. It's about the easiest machine there is on the market. It's certainly far less complicated than an espresso machine or even a waffle maker. In this chapter you'll learn about slow cookers and how to get the best results from them.

Slow cookers are inexpensive to operate; they use about as much electricity as a 60-watt bulb. They are also as easy to operate as flipping on a light switch.

Slow cookers operate by cooking food using indirect heat at a low temperature for an extended period of time. Here's the difference: Direct heat is the power of a stove burner underneath a pot, while indirect heat is the overall heat that surrounds foods as they bake in the oven.

You can purchase a slow cooker for as little as $20 at a discount store, while the top-of-the-line ones sell for more than $200. They all function in the same simple way; what increases the cost is the "bells and whistles" factors. Slow cookers come in both round and oval shapes, but they operate the same regardless of shape.

Food is assembled in a pottery insert that fits inside a metal housing and is topped with a clear lid. The food cooks from the heat generated by the circular heating wires encased between the slow cooker's outer and inner layers of metal. The coils never directly touch the crockery insert. As the element heats, it gently warms the air between the two layers of metal, and it is the hot air that touches the pottery. This construction method eliminates the need for stirring because no part of the pot gets hotter than any other.

On the front of this metal casing is the control knob. All slow cookers have Low and High settings, and most also have a Stay Warm position. Some new machines have a programmable option that enables you to start food on High and then the slow cooker automatically reduces the heat to Low after a programmed time.

The largest variation in slow cookers is their size, which range from tiny 1-quart models that are excellent for hot dips and fondue but fairly useless for anything else to gigantic 7-quart models that are excellent for large families and large batches.

> Rival introduced the first slow cooker, the Crock-Pot, in 1971, and the introductory slogan remains true more than 35 years later: It "cooks all day while the cook's away." Like such trademarked names as Kleenex for paper tissue or Formica for plastic laminate, Crock-Pot has almost become synonymous with the slow cooker. However, not all slow cookers are Crock-Pots, so the generic term is used in this book.

Most of the recipes in this book were written for and tested in a 4- or 5-quart slow cooker; that is what is meant by *medium.* Either of those sizes makes enough for four to eight people, depending on the recipe. In a few cases, such as for lamb shanks that take up a lot of room as they cook, a large slow cooker is specified.

Slow Cookers and Food Safety

Questions always arise as to the safety of slow cookers. The Food Safety and Inspection Service of the U.S. Department of Agriculture approves slow cooking as a method for safe food preparation. The lengthy cooking and the steam created within the tightly covered pot combine to destroy any bacteria that might be present in the food. But you do have to be careful.

It's far more common for food-borne illness to start with meat, poultry, and seafood than from contaminated fruits and vegetables. That is why it's not wise to cook whole chickens or cuts of meat larger than those specified in the recipes in this book because during slow cooking, these large items remain too long in the bacterial "danger zone"—between 40°F and 140°F. It is important that food reaches the higher temperature in less than two hours and remains at more than 140°F for at least 30 minutes.

Getting a jump-start on dinner while you're preparing breakfast may seem like a Herculean task, and it is possible to prep the ingredients destined for the slow cooker the night before—with some limitations. If you cut meat or vegetables in advance, store them separately in the refrigerator and layer them

> If you want to cook large roasts, brown them under the oven broiler or in a skillet on top of the stove over direct heat before you place them into the slow cooker. This will help the chilled meat heat up faster as well as produce a dish that is more visually appealing. Also begin with liquid that is boiling.

in the slow cooker in the morning. However, do not store the cooker insert in the refrigerator because that will also increase the amount of time it takes to heat the food to a temperature that kills bacteria.

Concern about food safety extends to after a meal is cooked and the leftovers are ready for storage. As long as the temperature remains 140°F or higher, food will stay safe for many hours in the slow cooker. Leftovers, however, should never be refrigerated in the crockery insert because it will take them too long to go through the "danger zone" in the other direction—from hot to cold.

Freeze or refrigerate leftovers in shallow containers within two hours after a dish has finished cooking. Also, food should never be reheated in the slow cooker because it takes too long for chilled food to reheat. Bacteria are a problem on cooked food as well as raw ingredients. The slow cooker can be used to keep food warm—and without the fear of burning it—once it has been reheated on the stove or in the oven.

One of the other concerns about food safety and the slow cooker is if there is a loss of power in the house—especially if you don't know when it occurred in the cooking process. If you're home, and

the amount of time was minimal, add it back into your end time. If the time without power increases to more than 30 minutes, finish the food by conventional cooking, adding more liquid, if necessary.

However, if you set the slow cooker before you left for work, and realize from electric clocks that power was off for more than an hour, it's best to discard the food, even if it looks done. You have no idea if the power outage occurred before the food passed through the "danger zone." Better safe than sorry.

> Always thaw food before placing it in the slow cooker to ensure the trip from 40°F to 140°F is accomplished quickly and efficiently. While adding a package of frozen green beans will slow up the cooking, starting with a frozen pot roast or chicken breast will make it impossible for the low temperature of the slow cooker to accomplish this task.

Slow Cooker Hints

Slow cookers can be perplexing if you're not accustomed to using one. Here are some general tips to help you master slow cooker conundrums:

* Remember that cooking times are wide approximations—within hours rather than minutes! That's because the age or power of a slow cooker as well as the temperature of ingredients must be taken into account. Check the food at the beginning of the stated cooking time, and then gauge whether it needs more time and about how much time. If carrots or cubes of potato are

still rock-hard, for example, turn the heat to High if cooking on Low, and realize that you're looking at another hour or so.

* Foods cook faster on the bottom of a slow cooker than at the top because there are more heat coils and they are totally immersed in the simmering liquid.

* Appliance manufacturers say that slow cookers can be left on either High or Low unattended, but use your own judgment. If you're going to be out of the house all day, it's advisable to cook food on Low. If, on the other hand, you're going to be gone for just a few hours, the food will be safe on High.

* Use leaf versions of dried herbs such as thyme and rosemary rather than ground versions. Ground herbs tend to lose potency during many hours in the slow cooker.

* If you want a sauce to have a more intense flavor, you can reduce the liquid in two ways. If cooking on Low, raise the heat to High, and remove the lid for the last hour of cooking. This will achieve some evaporation of the liquid. Or, remove the liquid either with a bulb baster or strain the liquid from the solids, and reduce them in a saucepan on the stove.

Slow Cooker Cautions

Slow cookers are benign, but they are electrical appliances with all the concomitant hazards of any machine plugged into a live wire. Be careful that the cord is not frayed in any way, and plug the slow cooker into an outlet that is not near the sink. Here are some tips on how to handle them:

* Never leave a slow cooker plugged in when not in use. It's all too easy to accidentally turn it on and not notice until the crockery insert cracks from overheating with nothing in it.

* Conversely, do not preheat the empty insert while you're preparing the food because the insert could crack when you add the cold food.

* Never submerge the metal casing in water or fill it with water. The inside of the metal does occasionally get dirty, but you can clean it quite well with an abrasive cleaner and then wipe it with a damp cloth or paper towel. While it's not aesthetically pleasing to see dirty metal, food never touches it, so if there are a few drips here and there it's not really important.

* Always remember that the insert is fragile, so don't drop it. Also, don't put a hot insert on a cold counter; that could cause it to break, too. The reverse is also true. While you can use the insert as a casserole in a conventional oven (assuming the lid is glass and not plastic), it cannot be put into a preheated oven if chilled.

* Resist the temptation to look and stir. Every time you take the lid off the slow cooker, you need to add 10 minutes of cooking time if cooking on High and 20 minutes if cooking on Low to compensate. Certain recipes in this book instruct you to add ingredients during the cooking time. In those cases the heat loss from opening the pot has been factored in to the total cooking time.

* Don't add more liquid to a slow cooker recipe than that specified in the recipe. Even if the food is not submerged in liquid when you start, foods such as meats and vegetables give off liquid as they cook; in the slow cooker, that additional liquid does not evaporate.

High-Altitude Adjustment

Rules for slow cooking, along with all other modes of cooking, change when the slow cooker is located more than 3,000 feet above sea level. At high altitudes the air is thinner so water boils at a lower temperature and comes to a boil more quickly. The rule is to always cook on High when above 3,000 feet; use the Low setting as a Keep Warm setting.

Other compensations are to reduce the liquid in a recipe by a few tablespoons and add about 5 to 10 percent more cooking time. The liquid may be bubbling, but it's not 212°F at first.

Converting Recipes for the Slow Cooker

Once you feel comfortable with your slow cooker, you'll probably want to use it to prepare your favorite recipes you now cook on the stove or in the oven. The best recipes to convert are "wet" ones with a lot of liquid, such as stews, soups, chilies, and other braised foods. Not all dishes can be easily converted to slow cooked dishes. Even if a dish calls for liquid, if it's supposed to be cooked or baked uncovered, chances are it will not be successfully transformed to a slow cooker recipe, because the food will not brown and the liquid will not evaporate.

The easiest way to convert your recipes is to find a similar one in this book and use its cooking time for guidance. When looking for a similar recipe, take into account the amount of liquid specified as well as the quantity of food. The liquid transfers the heat from the walls of the insert into the food itself, and the liquid heats in direct proportion to its measure.

You should look for similar recipes as well as keep in mind some general guidelines:

* Most any stew or roast takes 8 to 12 hours on Low and 4 to 6 hours on High.
* Chicken dishes cook more rapidly. Count on 6 to 8 hours on Low and 3 to 4 hours on High.
* Quadruple the time from conventional cooking to cooking on Low, and at least double it for cooking on High.
* Cut back on the amount of liquid used in stews and other braised dishes by about half. Unlike cooking on the stove or in the oven, there is little to no evaporation in the slow cooker.
* For soups, cut back on the liquid by one-third if the soup is supposed to simmer uncovered, and cut back by one-fourth if the soup is simmered covered. Even when covered, a soup that is simmering on the stove has more evaporation than one cooked in the slow cooker.

Modern slow cookers heat slightly hotter than those made thirty years ago; the Low setting on a slow cooker is about 200°F while the High setting is close to 300°F. If you have a vintage appliance, it's a good idea to test it to make sure it still has the power to heat food sufficiently. Leave 2 quarts water at room temperature overnight, and then pour the water into the slow cooker in the morning. Heat it on Low for 8 hours. The temperature should be 185°F after 8 hours. Use an instant read thermometer to judge it. If it is lower, any food you cook in this cooker might not pass through the danger zone rapidly enough.

Chapter 3

Breakfast Paleo-Style

*O*ne can't be a fully engaged hunter-gatherer without breakfast, so no Paleo diet is complete without it. You may be coming off of a typical American breakfast featuring a grain/dairy pairing like buttered bread or toast, cereal with milk, pancakes, even oatmeal. While you might be enjoying meats, eggs, or even fruit with that, chances are the grain and dairy items are the standouts in your morning breakfast routine. Well, it's time to change that.

It might seem impossible—and trust us, it won't be easy—but it is possible. And not only is it possible, but it's pretty darn satisfying and tasty, too. Like changing any habit, what you'll miss is more the routine of it. You'll be surprised in the first few weeks of your changeover to Paleo by how often you think of or reach for a non-Paleo food. But keep your mind on what you *can* eat on the Paleo diet, and you'll be surprised by how many options you have.

The easiest breakfast choices for Paleos are simple things that take little time to prepare, such as eggs, fruit, and omelets with meat and vegetables. This cookbook is about using the slow cooker, though, so the recipes in it are for more leisurely times or when you need to plan ahead. There are great options for weekends, as well as for make-aheads for really tight schedules.

One of our favorite recipes is the very first one, which is for hard-boiled eggs. What a delight to know you can put a dozen eggs in your slow cooker, cover them with water, turn it on, go watch a movie or play games with your family, and in a couple of hours, they're done! Take them out, refrigerate them, and you have yummy cooked eggs ready for you in the morning. Enjoy!

Slow-Cooked Eggs

This is as simple as it gets. Unlike hard-boiling your eggs on the stovetop, you don't have to worry about the water boiling over.

Cooks up to a dozen eggs.

8 to 12 eggs (depending on how many fit in one layer on the bottom of your slow cooker)

Large bowl of ice water

1. Place the eggs gently on the bottom of the slow cooker, being sure they are in a single layer. Add tap water to cover. Cover and cook on High for 2 hours.

2. When cooked, remove with tongs and place into bowl of ice water. Let the eggs stay in the ice bath for a couple of minutes. This reduces the temperature and loosens the shell for easy peeling.

> Hard-boiled eggs make great Paleo snacks. Sprinkle with black pepper, garlic powder, paprika, or even a splash of hot sauce. Enjoy!

Egg Bake with Spinach and Mushrooms

This dish will feed a crowd—or you for a couple of days, which isn't such a bad thing!

Serves 10 to 12.

2 tablespoons olive oil

1 cup sliced domestic mushrooms

1 onion, chopped fine

4 cups spinach leaves, coarse stems removed, and ripped or cut into smaller pieces

12 eggs

1 cup coconut milk

1 tablespoon chopped fresh parsley

Salt and pepper to taste

1. Lightly grease the inside of the slow cooker with a teaspoon of the olive oil.

2. In large skillet, cook onion and mushrooms in remainder of olive oil until tender. Turn the heat off, place the spinach leaves over the mixture, and cover with a tight-fitting lid. Allow the spinach to steam under the lid for about 10 minutes, which will cause it to wilt.

3. In a large bowl, beat the eggs and coconut milk until well mixed. Add the onion, mushroom, and spinach mixture, then the parsley, and stir just to combine.

4. Pour the eggs and vegetables into the slow cooker, cover and turn on Low. Cook on Low for 1 to 2 hours, until eggs are thoroughly cooked. To test for doneness, insert a clean knife in the center. If it comes out clean, the dish is ready.

This is delicious served with a fresh salsa. Chop 2 very ripe tomatoes and put them in a small bowl. Add a squirt of lime juice, a tablespoon of finely minced onion, 1 clove of crushed garlic, and a teaspoon or so of chopped jalapeno pepper (or a spicy pepper of your choice). Season with pepper and just a dash of salt.

Broccoli Frittata

This makes a colorful and nutritious baked egg dish.

Serves 6.

2 tablespoons olive oil

1 medium onion, chopped

2 cloves garlic, minced

½ red or green bell pepper,
seeds and ribs removed, thinly sliced

8 large eggs

3 tablespoons water

2 tablespoons fresh chopped parsley

1 tablespoon fresh thyme

¾ cup fresh broccoli florets,
cut into bite-sized pieces

1. Heat the olive oil in a skillet and add onion, garlic, and red pepper. Cook over medium-high heat until onion is translucent, about 3 minutes.

2. In a large bowl, whisk eggs with water, then add herbs and broccoli pieces. Add the cooked vegetables. Take a large piece of parchment paper, fold it in half, and place it in the slow cooker so the sides come up the sides of the cooker. This will give you a way to lift out the egg dish when it is cooked. Pour the egg mixture in on top of the parchment paper.

3. Cover and cook on High for 1 to 2 hours or on Low for 2 to 3 hours until eggs are set.

4. Run a spatula along the sides of the cooker to loosen the parchment paper. Lift the frittata out of the cooker with the paper, and slide it onto a serving plate.

Broccoli is a vegetable loaded with Vitamin C and dietary fiber. If yours is a family that happens to love it, lucky you! It's versatile, filling, and really good for you!

Garden Vegetable Eggs

Besides making a wonderful breakfast, this colorful egg dish can also be served as a light lunch or dinner with a big salad—using some of the same vegetables!

Serves 6 to 8.

2 tablespoons olive oil

1 onion, chopped fine

1 small zucchini, chopped

1 small yellow pepper, deseeded and chopped

2 ripe plum tomatoes, chopped

¼ cup chopped fresh basil

8 eggs

½ cup water

Salt and pepper to taste

1. Lightly grease the inside of the slow cooker with a teaspoon of the olive oil.

2. In large skillet, cook onion, zucchini, and pepper until just tender, about 5 minutes. Add the tomatoes and basil and stir to heat through. Remove from heat.

3. In a large bowl, beat the eggs and water until well mixed. Add the vegetable mixture, and stir just to combine.

4. Pour the eggs and vegetables into the slow cooker. Cover and cook on Low for 2 to 3 hours, until eggs are thoroughly cooked. To test for doneness, insert a clean knife in the center. If it comes out clean, the dish is ready.

Variation:

✳ Create a Paleo eggs Benedict by serving this yummy egg dish on top of a piece of grilled Canadian bacon. Garnish with a sprig of basil or parsley for Sunday brunch elegance.

Bacon Spread

This intense savory spread is the perfect antidote to a bland breakfast. Spoon it onto slices of hardboiled egg for a whole new breakfast treat.

Makes about 1 cup, and stores in the refrigerator for several weeks.

2 pounds thick sliced bacon, cut crosswise into 1-inch pieces

2 medium onions, diced

3 garlic cloves, peeled and sliced thin

½ cup cider vinegar

½ cup honey, preferably dark amber

1 teaspoon cocoa powder

1 tablespoon water, if necessary

1. In a large skillet over medium-high heat, cook the bacon about 20 minutes, or until the meat is browned and the fat is mostly rendered. Scoop out the bacon with a slotted spoon, transferring it onto a plate lined with paper towels.

2. Saving 1 tablespoon of the bacon grease, pour the rest out of the skillet. Heat the bacon grease, and add the onions and garlic, stirring frequently and cooking until tender and translucent, about 4 minutes. Add vinegar, honey, and cocoa powder, and stir. If paste is too thick, add water 1 tablespoon at a time so that there is some moisture in the pan. When the sauce is just boiling, add the bacon, stir to combine, and remove from heat.

3. Transfer mixture to a slow cooker. Leaving it uncovered, cook on High for 3 to 4 hours, or until the liquid has thickened and is syrupy. As mixture cools, break bacon up into smaller bits. Serve immediately, or store in an airtight container for later use.

> Although bacon is Paleo-friendly food, buying poor-quality, fatty cuts in the grocery store is not the healthiest of eating habits. The thick-cut bacon prepared by a local farmer is the much better choice.

Early Riser Poached Salmon

In many cultures, fish is a breakfast of champions. Smoked salmon with cream cheese and bagels is a popular brunch menu selection. But for Paleo people, this poached salmon kicks the excess calories of the other combo to the curb. For good.

Makes 4 to 6 servings.

6 cups water

1 medium onion, chopped

2 stalks celery, chopped

4 sprigs parsley

½ cup freshly squeezed lemon juice

8 whole black peppercorns

1 bay leaf

1 5-pound fillet or 4 small steaks of salmon

1 small lemon, sliced, for garnish

2 tablespoons fresh parsley, chopped, for garnish

1. To make the poaching liquid, combine water, onion, celery, parsley, lemon juice, peppercorns, and bay leaf over medium heat. Bring to a boil and simmer for 30 minutes. Strain and discard solids.

2. Take a large sheet of heavy duty aluminum foil and place it inside the slow cooker so the sides emerge over the top. Press it into place so it conforms with the inside of the cooker. Turn the cooker on to High and, uncovered, let it preheat. Place the salmon over the foil in the slow cooker. Pour the hot poaching liquid over the salmon. Cover immediately, and cook on High for 1 to 2 hours until the flesh of the salmon is cooked through to a light pink but firm color and consistency.

3. Remove stoneware from slow cooker. Allow salmon to cool for 20 minute before transferring to a platter and serving. Garnish with lemon slices and fresh parsley sprigs.

This is a really tasty and satisfying breakfast after a workout—especially an early morning run. To come home to a fragrant, succulent piece of hot salmon is so much more enjoyable than a cold buttered bagel!

Baked Apples and Pears

When these fruits are fresh in the fall, with a cold nip in the air, this is a breakfast treat that can't be beat.

Makes 4 to 8 servings.

2 tablespoons dried red currants, cranberries, or sour cherries

2 tablespoons honey

½ cup chopped macadamia nuts

½ teaspoon cinnamon

½ teaspoon nutmeg

½ teaspoon ginger

2 tablespoons coconut oil

4 large, firm-fleshed apples, cored

4 large pears, small tops removed, and cored

¼ cup apple or pear cider

1. In a small bowl, combine the dried fruit, honey, nuts, ¼ teaspoon each of the cinnamon, nutmeg, and ginger, and 1 tablespoon of the coconut oil.

2. Position the apples and pears in the bottom of the slow cooker, bottoms down, and carefully spoon the fruit/nut combo into the openings.

3. Melt the additional tablespoon of coconut oil in a small skillet over low heat, add the remaining ¼ teaspoons of the spices, and, warming the spices. Pour the oil-and-spice mixture over the fruits. Pour the apple or pear cider into the slow cooker along the side so it goes to the bottom.

4. Cover and cook 3 to 4 hours on Low or 2 to 3 hours on High or until fruit is tender. Serve warm or at room temperature.

> These baked fruits make a wonderful addition to a full Paleo breakfast of eggs and meat. Or, with a side salad, they are the complementary dessert to a lovely weekend brunch.

Hearty and Hot Almond Meal

If you crave a breakfast cereal, this delicious porridge-y almond meal recipe is sure to hit the spot.

Makes 4 to 6 servings.

2 cups peeled and chopped apples

4 cups almond meal

4 cups water

½ teaspoon cinnamon

½ teaspoon nutmeg

1. Place the chopped fruit in the bottom of the slow cooker. Add the almond meal, water, cinnamon, and nutmeg. Stir to combine.

2. Cover and cook on Low for 5 to 6 hours until all water is absorbed and the fruit is tender.

Variation:

∗ Try adding dried fruits such as cranberries, currants, or raisins. Either cook them with the cereal or add sprinkle them on top when the cereal is cooked.

Chapter 4

Paleo Treats and Nibbles

*T*his is a fun section of the book, because it's full of yummy things you can munch on as finger foods in between meals.

The variety of treats and nibbles you can make with a full Paleo-approved palette is really limited only by your imagination and what's in your cupboard. In this chapter, you'll find everything from great party foods like hot dogs wrapped in bacon, spiced pistachios, curried cauliflower, or sweet potato wedges, to mini meals like lamb kabobs, fish bites, and meatballs.

Another thing you'll find as you immerse yourself in the Paleo diet is that you really don't need to eat as much as you may have been accustomed to eating. When you prepare some of these nibbler dishes and put them on pretty plates with some crudités around them to dress them up, and eat them with toothpicks or cocktail forks, you'll find yourself filling up and feeling more satisfied than if you were wolfing down a meatball parmesan sub, for example.

Experiment with flavors, textures, types of meat or fish used, and sauces, and you'll discover a wealth of treats for the new Paleo you.

Hot Dog and Bacon Bites

These are fun to make for any kind of party—or for after-school snacks for hungry teenagers. The best hot dogs are those made from grass-fed meat.

Makes 10 to 12 party servings.

2 pounds all-beef hot dogs

1 pound thick-cut bacon

Honey to drizzle

1. Slice hot dogs in half crosswise. Separate the bacon slices and cut them in half crosswise, as well. Wrap each hot dog half with a bacon strip, and fasten with toothpicks at the top and bottom.

2. Layer the wrapped hot dogs in the slow cooker, drizzling each layer lightly with honey. Repeat layers until hot dogs run out.

3. Cover and cook on Low for 3 to 4 hours. Remove with tongs, slice into bite-sized pieces, and put a toothpick into every piece to secure the bacon and make for easy eating.

Variation:

✳ In lieu of hotdogs, try fresh kielbasa! It makes for thicker bites than the hot dogs. You'll need to cut the sausage into 3- to 4-inch pieces as well as slicing it in half crosswise.

Chicken Nuggets

You will be delighted by these seasoned chicken bites. They are so much healthier than the frozen nuggets so common in our fast-food cuisine.

Makes 6 to 8 party servings.

1 pound boneless skinless chicken breast or thigh

¼ cup olive oil

1 teaspoon fresh parsley, minced

2 garlic cloves, minced

1 teaspoon lemon zest

1 teaspoon onion powder

½ teaspoon cayenne

¼ teaspoon salt

¼ teaspoon pepper

1. If the chicken breasts are particularly thick, place them between sheets of waxed paper and pound them to about ½-inch thickness with a mallet or rolling pin. Cut the chicken into "nugget" sizes.

2. In a large bowl, combine olive oil with parsley, garlic, lemon zest, onion powder, cayenne, salt, and pepper. Stir or whisk to combine well.

3. Put the chicken pieces in the bowl, and stir to coat. If desired, the chicken can marinate in the oil mixture for up to 30 minutes in the refrigerator, but this isn't necessary.

4. Place the chicken in the slow cooker with the additional oil mixture. Cover and cook on Low for 4 to 6 hours or on High for 2 to 3 hours. In the last half hour of cooking, prop open the lid with the handle of a wooden spoon so some steam is released and the nuggets dry a little.

Serve these with a Paleo-approved dipping sauce or condiment (see the Paleo Pantry chapter for ideas), or squeeze fresh lemon over them and some chopped fresh parsley.

Baba Ghanoush

This is an eggplant dip that also makes a great spread on large lettuce leaves when making wraps of any kind. Or you could do what I do, which is just eat it by the spoonful!

Makes about 2 cups.

1 large eggplant

4 cloves garlic, chopped

1 tablespoon olive oil

2 tablespoons tahini (raw, not roasted)

2 tablespoons fresh-squeezed lemon juice

1 teaspoon tomato paste

1 teaspoon salt

¼ teaspoon pepper

¼ teaspoon cayenne (optional)

1. Cut the very top off of the eggplant. Slice it into quarters, and peel the skin off with a paring knife.

2. In a bowl, combine the garlic, olive oil, tahini, lemon juice, tomato paste, salt, pepper, and cayenne.

3. Place the eggplant in the slow cooker and pour the oil mix over it. Cover and cook on Low for 3 to 4 hours. Mash with a fork before serving.

Tahini is a paste made from sesame seeds, which are a Paleo-friendly food. Find a raw tahini in your health food store, if possible, and buy only a small quantity. It's the processing of the seeds for commercial tahinis that can tarnish the nutritive value of the paste.

Pork Meatballs

These are always a hit at parties. There's something that's just fun about meatballs. Make them for regular meals, too, to lighten up a weeknight dinner.

Makes about 24 small meatballs.

2 pounds ground pork

1 apple, peeled, cored, and grated

2 teaspoon fresh sage, chopped fine

2 teaspoon fresh thyme, chopped fine

1 teaspoon ground fennel seeds

2 large eggs, beaten

¼ onion, minced fine

2 cloves garlic, minced

1 tablespoon coconut oil

Salt and pepper to taste

1. In a large bowl, combine the pork, grated apple, sage, thyme, fennel seeds, eggs, onion, and garlic. Stir to combine well. Form the meat mixture into meatballs and set aside on a plate.

2. In a large skillet, heat coconut oil over medium-high heat to melting. Add the meatballs (in batches if necessary) and turn them so they brown on all sides. Using a slotted spoon, transfer the browned meatballs to the slow cooker.

3. Cover and cook on Low for 3 to 4 hours, or on High for 2 to 3 hours. Sprinkle with salt and pepper before serving.

Applesauce is a great accompaniment to pork, and these meatballs are no exception! Serve them hot with chunky applesauce that's at room temperature.

Leafy Chicken Wraps

A wrap is really just a way to contain the food that's inside it. While we think of wraps as being made of pastry or grains, a leaf of a fresh green makes for an equally appropriate container—and truthfully much more flavorful.

Makes 10 to 12 wraps.

4 boneless skinless chicken breasts or thighs

2 tablespoons olive oil

3 cloves garlic, minced

¼ onion, minced

1 large carrot, coarsely chopped

1 tablespoon fresh-squeezed lemon juice

1 teaspoon lemon zest

1 tablespoon fresh parsley, minced

1 6- or 8-oz jar artichoke hearts packed in oil, drained

1 head Romaine lettuce

1. Cut the chicken into bite-sized pieces and put it in the slow cooker.

2. In a bowl, combine the olive oil, garlic, onion, carrot, lemon juice, zest, and parsley. Pour over chicken.

3. Cover and cook on Low for 5 to 6 hours or on High for 3 to 4 hours. In the last hour of cooking, add the artichoke hearts and stir to combine. Continue cooking for the desired time, or until chicken is very tender. Stir the mix, and pull the chicken apart with a fork. Allow to cool.

4. Wash and dry 10 to 12 large Romaine leaves. Put a scoop of the shredded chicken mix onto a leaf and roll it up. Secure with a toothpick.

Variations:
There are lots of foods you can include with the chicken mixture to enhance the flavor and texture of these wraps. Try:
* Sliced almonds, toasted
* Chopped celery
* Chopped red peppers
* Green or red seedless grapes, cut in half
* Spicy pepitas
* Chopped parsley
* Chopped cilantro

Devils on Horseback

Here's a slow-cooker take on the classic cocktail party food of the 1970s, which is still very popular today. Be sure to crack the lid on the slow cooker as directed so the bacon gets a bit crispy.

Makes 24 "devils."

24 large dates, pitted

12 slices thick-cut bacon, halved

Toothpicks

Wrap each date in a piece of bacon and secure with a toothpick. Place the "devils" in the slow cooker. Their sides can touch. Cover and cook on High for 3 to 4 hours. During the last hour, prop the lid open with the handle of a wooden spoon. This allows the steam to escape and makes the snacks crispier. Serve hot.

Variations:

✻ If you want an extra layer of flavor, consider drizzling the wraps with a tiny bit of honey—just enough for a drop or two per wrap. For an extra zing, you can also sprinkle them lightly with cayenne or curry powder during the last hour of cooking when the lid is ajar.

Chicken Wings

For a really fun party, challenge your Paleo-friendly neighbors and friends to a chicken wing cook-off. There are so many great ways to prepare these; this recipe is along traditional lines.

Serves 6 to 8.

2 to 3 lbs chicken wings

½ cup coconut milk

2 tablespoons Asian red chili sauce, such as Sriracha

2 cloves garlic, minced

1. Heat oven to 450F. Line a cookie sheet with parchment paper. Put the wings on it and cook for about 10 minutes, turning once.

2. Put the wings in the slow cooker. In a bowl, combine other ingredients and pour over the wings.

3. Cover and cook on Low for 4 to 5 hours or on High for 3 to 4 hours.

4. When cooked through, the wings can be crisp-finished by putting them on a cookie sheet lined with parchment paper and baked in a 400F oven for about 10 minutes.

When these wings are ready, you'll love the extra slow-cooked dipping sauce.

Beef Tongue Yum with Avocado Salsa

For those who've never tried tongue before, you are in for an amazing treat! If the idea of it doesn't sit so well with you, take out the word "tongue," and call it Beef Yum instead. Think of your Paleo ancestors, for whom this cut was one of the very best parts of the beast.

Serves 10 to 12.

1 beef tongue

1 onion, sliced

3 garlic cloves, crushed

3 bay leaves

salt and pepper

Cold water to cover

FOR THE AVOCADO SALSA:

1 avocado, peeled, pitted, and cut into chunks

2 ripe tomatoes, diced, seeds removed

½ jalapeno pepper, seeds removed and chopped fine

1 tablespoon lime juice

1. Wash the tongue with cold water and pat it dry.

2. Put the onion slices, crushed garlic, and bay leaves in the bottom of the slow cooker, and place the tongue on top. Season with salt and pepper. Gently pour water into the slow cooker until the tongue is completely submerged. Cover and cook on Low for 7 to 8 hours or on High for 5 to 6 hours.

3. Remove the tongue and peel off the skin.

4. Put the avocado, tomatoes, jalapeno pepper, and lime juice in a bowl and combine. Serve the avocado salsa with the shredded tongue.

> This is a great filling for leafy wraps, too. Use Romaine leaves or iceburg lettuce or endive.

Teriyaki Turkey Meatballs

Spicy and succulent, these are delicious nibblers which, like the other meatball recipes, make for fun snacks and meals.

Makes about 14 meatballs.

1 lb ground turkey

½ teaspoon cayenne

2 slices fresh pineapple, minced

1 tablespoon coconut aminos

1 clove garlic, minced

1 tablespoon fresh ginger, grated

1 egg, lightly beaten

1 tablespoon olive oil

1. In a large bowl, combine all ingredients except the olive oil. Form into meatballs.

2. Put 1 tablespoon oil in a large skillet over medium-high heat, and add the meatballs, turning to brown on all sides. Put browned meatballs in the slow cooker. Cover and cook on Low for 5 to 6 hours or on High for 4 to 5 hours.

If serving for a party, put the meatballs on a platter with a dish in the center filled with the juice from the slow cooker. It makes a great dipping *jus*. Be sure to have toothpicks in the meatballs when serving.

Party Portobellos

There's nothing like a big slice of slow-cooked Portobello mushroom, when the flavor explodes with every bite. This is another so-simple but so satisfying recipe that can easily be doubled to make extra. You'll want to be able to quickly reheat them to enjoy through the week.

Makes about 2 cups cooked Portobellos.

3 large Portobello mushrooms, loose, or 16 to 18 oz packaged Portobellos

3 tablespoons olive oil

3 tablespoons ghee or clarified butter

Salt and pepper to taste

Chopped rosemary or dill for garnish, if desired

1. Go over the Portobellos and remove any obvious dirt by brushing or shaking it off. Slice the Portobellos into thick slices (¼-inch or so). Put the slices into the slow cooker.

2. In a small skillet, heat the olive oil and ghee over medium heat until melted and combined. Pour the melted oil/butter combination over the Portobellos.

3. Cover and cook on Low for 3 to 4 hours or on High for 1 to 2 hours. The mushrooms should be cooked through but not too mushy. Season lightly with salt and pepper before serving, and if desired, garnish with rosemary or dill in the serving dish. Be sure to have toothpicks available to eat them at a party.

> The Portobello mushroom is an oversized crimini mushroom. Both are dark-brown mushrooms related to the common mushroom. Creminis and Portobellos share a mustier, earthier flavor as well as color from the common white mushroom. Large Portobellos are so meaty that they are often cooked as meat substitutes, making great "burgers" for vegetarians.

BBQ Riblets

The fat content of pork ribs makes them especially juicy and tasty. When slow cooked then topped with a delectable, tangy, Paleo-approved BBQ sauce, all you need in addition is a side salad and lots of napkins.

Serves 4 to 6.

2 to 3 racks of baby back pork ribs, cut into small pieces

Salt and pepper

6-oz can tomato paste

½ cup water

2 tablespoons cider vinegar

2 teaspoon honey

¼ teaspoon dry mustard

1 teaspoon Asian red chili sauce, such as Sriracha

½ teaspoon ground pepper

1. Cut the ribs into individual pieces, as close to bite size as possible (though this isn't necessary for the cooking time). Put them in a colander and wash them with cold water, then pat them dry.

2. Place the ribs in the slow cooker. Cover and cook on Low for 6 to 8 hours or on High for 5 to 6 hours.

3. While ribs are cooking, combine tomato paste, water, cider vinegar, honey, mustard, chili sauce, and pepper in a saucepan. Heat over medium heat and stir while bringing to a boil. Turn heat to low and simmer for about 5 minutes.

4. In the last hour of cooking, add the barbeque sauce and continue until the ribs are thoroughly cooked.

This cooking method and recipe make a lot of sauce and juice. To reduce it to a thick "gravy" for the cooked riblets, use a baster to remove a lot of the fat that has risen to the surface while cooking. Transfer the ribs to a platter and keep warm in the oven. Put the sauce from the slow cooker into a saucepan on the stove and cook over medium heat, stirring to blend and reduce. If you want to thicken the sauce, combine 1 teaspoon of arrowroot with ¼ cup of the hot liquid, stir thoroughly, then stir back into the sauce and continue to stir until thickened, about 10 minutes.

Sweet Potato Wedges

Sweet potatoes—rich in Vitamin A, beta-carotene, and an assortment of minerals—have been rapidly replacing the white potato in lots of recipes, including French fries, which is the basis of this snack.

Serves 4 to 6.

4 medium-sized sweet potatoes, peeled and sliced into thin wedges

½ cup water

4 tablespoons coconut oil

Salt and pepper

Cayenne pepper (optional)

Onion powder (optional)

1. Place the sweet potato wedges into the slow cooker. Add the water. Drizzle the sweet potatoes with the oil. Cover and cook on Low for 4 to 5 hours or on High for 2 to 3 hours.

2. Prop open the lid with the handle of a wooden spoon, and continue to cook another 30 minutes or so on High to get some browning.

3. When ready to serve, season with salt and pepper—and some cayenne and onion powder if you want something spicier.

Variation:
You can use other hearty, Paleo-appropriate veggies for this dish:
* Turnips, dusted with cumin and paprika
* Thick carrot wedges seasoned with lemon, salt, and dill
* Beets with a hint of maple sugar

Paleo Escargot

Like fish, snails are high in protein and low in fat. Considered a delicacy in many parts of the world, and best known as the French preparation, *escargot*—prepared in butter, garlic, and parsley—they make a very tasty slow-cooked snack.

Serves 4.

2 7.75-oz cans of Roland large snails (24 total)

4 tablespoons ghee

4 cloves garlic, crushed in a garlic press

2 tablespoons fresh parsley, chopped

Salt and pepper

1. Drain and rinse the snails.

2. In a skillet over medium heat, melt the ghee. Add the garlic, stirring until fragrant, about 2 minutes.

3. Add the snails and continue to cook until coated with the ghee/garlic, about 2 minutes.

4. Add the parsley, remove from the heat, stir, and transfer to the slow cooker. Cook on Low for 40 to 60 minutes until heated through.

5. Season with salt and pepper. Serve with toothpicks and a side dish of the garlic sauce, or wrap a few in a lettuce leaf.

If you want to pretend you're in a French cooking class, while the snails are still hot in the slow cooker, pour in ¼ cup Vermouth. Shake to distribute, then light a match over the cooker to light the alcohol on fire. It will burn for just a minute, leaving behind the flavor.

Lamb Kabobs

You'll be eager to eat these when you smell them cooking. This is a recipe full of Mediterranean goodness.

Makes 6 to 10 kabobs.

½ cup olive oil

1 teaspoon rosemary, minced

3 cloves garlic, minced

¼ teaspoon each salt and pepper

1 pound boneless leg of lamb, cubed

2 red bell peppers, cored and seeded, cut into chunks

1 onion, peeled and cut into small wedges

1 large zucchini, cut into thick slices

Wooden skewer sticks, broken to fit the length of the slow cooker

1. In a large bowl, combine the olive oil, rosemary, garlic, and salt and pepper.

2. Add the lamb cubes and stir to coat.

3. Using the wooden skewers, make kabobs alternating lamb, peppers, onions, and zucchini.

4. Lay the kabobs in the slow cooker, and pour the remaining oil mixture over them. Cover and cook on Low for 3 to 4 hours or on High for 1 to 2 hours until lamb is cooked through and vegetables have softened. Baste with juices from the slow cooker before serving.

These are delicious dipped in Mint Sauce (page 19). You can also sandwich a kabob in a lettuce leaf and top with some Baba Ghanoush (page 51).

Chapter 5

Soups and Stews

*I*f you're relatively new to the Paleo diet and lifestyle, and you're relatively new to slow cooking, this chapter should be your starting point. It features recipes with a great assortment of Paleo staples like meat, fish, and vegetables. And, of course, all these recipes are made in the slow cooker, which is ideal for soups and stews. In fact, you almost can't go wrong making a soup or stew in the slow cooker when you get the feel for quantities of solids and liquids, because the slow-cooking process renders foods into these liquid-rich, deliciously satisfying meals.

The biggest difference between Paleo soups and stews and those of more traditional diets is the absence of grains and, often, of dairy to make a soup creamy. When you learn to substitute vegetables that are great grain substitutes, like cauliflower or sweet potatoes or others that thicken and enhance, you won't miss the addition of pasta or rice or even regular potatoes. As for making something creamy, it is Paleo-appropriate to use coconut milk, and you'll discover how to do this.

In this chapter you'll also find recipes for meat, fish, and vegetable broths that are the cornerstones of the best Paleo diets. Using real bones, vegetables, and spices, as described here, creates broths that are loaded with nutrients. Many of the recipes in this book call for the addition of a broth, and if you use one that's homemade, you will be doing a world of good for your body.

Chicken Stock

Besides being the base of so many recipes, homemade stock is in and of itself an amazing food. Made with all parts of the chicken (or beef, or fish), a slow-cooked stock is rich in many minerals essential to good health, including calcium, magnesium, phosphorous, silicon, sulphur, and even glucosamine and chondroitin, which we often pay a lot of money for as a supplement for joint care! It is prized around the world as a remedy for whatever ails you, from digestive upset to sore throats to low libido. Note: The amounts in this recipe are for a larger slow cooker; if yours is small, cut the recipe in half.

Makes about 12 cups.

1 whole free-range chicken,
or 2 to 3 pounds of the bony parts
(necks, backs, breastbones, legs, wings)

Gizzards from the chicken

2 to 4 chicken feet (optional but beneficial)

1 large onion, chopped

2 carrots, peeled and sliced

2 celery stalks, chopped

4 quarts cold water

2 tablespoons vinegar

1 bunch parsley, chopped

1. If you are using a whole chicken, cut off the neck, wings, and legs and cut them into pieces. Cut the rest of the chicken pieces into chunks.

2. Place chicken pieces in the slow cooker and top with all vegetables except the parsley. Cover with water and vinegar. Cover, and let the meat and vegetables sit in the liquid for 30 minutes to 1 hour.

3. Turn the slow cooker to High and cook for 2 to 3 hours, or until boiling. Remove the cover and spoon off and discard any scum that has risen to the top.

4. Replace the cover and reduce the heat to Low. Cook for 8 to 10 hours. Add the parsley in the last 15 minutes or so.

5. When cooking is complete, remove the solids with a slotted spoon into a colander over a bowl. Any drippings in the bowl can go back into the stock. Remove any meat from the bones and eat separately.

6. Transfer the stock to a large bowl and refrigerate. When the fat is congealed on top, remove it, and transfer the stock to several smaller containers with tight-fitting lids. Stock can be stored in the refrigerator for several days, or kept frozen.

For a browner, even richer stock, place the chicken pieces on a cookie sheet. Preheat the oven broiler, and broil for about 3 minutes per side, until browned.

Beef Stock

This stock will add new layers of delicious complexity to the recipes it's in—and will make your kitchen smell fantastic while it's cooking.

Makes about 10 cups.

2 lbs beef marrow bones
2 lbs meaty rib or neck bones
3 quarts water
¼ cup vinegar
1 large onion, chopped
2 large carrots, chopped
2 celery stalks, chopped
3 sprigs of fresh thyme
1 teaspoon peppercorns
1 bunch parsley

1. Place the beef bones in a large pot and cover with water and vinegar. Let stand for 1 hour.

2. Place the meaty bones in a roasting pan. Preheat the oven to 350 and roast until well browned, about 30 to 40 minutes.

3. Place the soaked beef bones and the browned pieces in the slow cooker. Add the onion, carrot, celery, thyme, and peppercorns, and cover with the water.

4. Discard the fat from the roasting pan, and fill with an inch or so of water. Place the pan over a burner on medium-high heat, and as the water heats, stir to loosen the coagulated juices and browned bits. Add this to the slow cooker. The water should just cover the meat and vegetables; add more if it doesn't.

5. Turn the slow cooker on High and cook for 2 to 3 hours until liquid is boiling. Remove lid and scoop out and discard any scum that has risen to the top.

6. Replace the lid, lower the heat to Low, and cook for 12 to 18 hours— the longer, the better. Add the parsley during the last 15 minutes.

7. When cooking is complete, remove the solids with a slotted spoon into a colander over a bowl. Any drippings in the bowl can go back into the stock. Remove any meat from the bones and eat separately.

8. Transfer the stock to a large bowl and refrigerate. When the fat is congealed on top, remove it, and transfer the stock to several smaller containers with tight-fitting lids. Stock can be stored in the refrigerator for several days, or kept frozen.

> **Making broths is Paleo at its purest. After all, nothing was wasted from a slaughtered animal in Paleolithic times— and even still in many parts of the world. The nutrients extracted from the slow-cooking process are easily absorbed by the body. It's wonderful to get so much goodness out of parts we might normally discard.**

Vegetable Stock

Even if you're cooking a vegetarian dish, start with the vegetable stock rather than adding more vegetables to the dish. It creates the background for all other flavors.

Makes about 6 cups.

2 quarts boiling water

2 carrots, thinly sliced

2 stalks celery, chopped

2 large leeks, white parts only, thinly sliced

1 small onion, thinly sliced

1 tablespoon black peppercorns

2 cloves garlic, peeled

3 sprigs thyme

1 bay leaf

1 bunch parsley

1. Pour boiling water into the slow cooker, and add carrots, celery, leeks, onion, peppercorns, garlic, thyme, and bay leaf. Cook on low for 6 to 8 hours or on High for 4 to 5 hours. Add parsley the final 15 minutes of cooking time.

2. Strain stock through a sieve into a large mixing bowl. Press down on the solids with the back of a spoon to extract as much liquid as possible. Discard solids.

3. Refrigerate the stock. Stock can be stored in the refrigerator for several days, or kept frozen.

> Save the water you use when boiling or steaming mildly flavored vegetables such as spinach, carrots or green beans, and make them part of the liquid used for the stock. However, the water from any member of the cabbage family, like broccoli or cauliflower, is too strong.

Fish Stock

The carcasses of fish typically have the filets removed already. If you can find a good fishmonger near you, he or she should have plenty to sell you at a modest price. Be sure to get the heads, too, as they are rich in iodine and fat-soluble vitamins.

Makes about 10 cups.

2 tablespoons clarified butter

2 onions, chopped

1 carrot, chopped

½ cup dry vermouth

2 or 3 whole carcasses from non-oily fish such as snapper, rockfish, sole or cod

3 sprigs fresh thyme

Several sprigs fresh parsley

1 bay leaf

¼ cup vinegar

3 quarts cold water

1. In a large skillet over medium heat, melt butter and add onions and carrots. Cook for a couple of minutes at the higher heat to coat the vegetables, then reduce the heat to low and cook, stirring occasionally, until vegetables are soft, about 30 minutes. Add the vermouth and increase the heat to bring to a near boil.

2. Place the carcasses in the slow cooker. Cover with the water and vinegar. Add the vegetable mixture, thyme, parsley, and bay leaf.

3. Cover and cook on High for 4 to 5 hours until liquid is boiling. Remove the cover and scoop off and discard the scum that has risen to the top.

4. Replace the cover and cook on Low for 10 to 18 hours—the longer the better.

5. When cooking is complete, remove the solids with a slotted spoon. Transfer the stock to a large bowl and refrigerate. When the fat is congealed on top, remove it, and transfer the stock to several smaller containers with tight-fitting lids. Stock can be stored in the refrigerator for several days, or kept frozen.

Variation:

✳ To make **Seafood Stock,** skip the first and use lobster bodies from which the claws and tail have been removed. With this recipe, use either 3 to 4 lobster bodies, or the bodies of 2 lobsters and the shells from 2 to 4 pounds of raw shrimp.

Chicken Soup with Fennel and Escarole

The licorice flavor of fresh fennel is reinforced by fennel seeds in this easy Italian healthful chicken soup.

Serves 6 to 8.

1 lb boneless, skinless chicken breasts

1 large fennel bulb

3 tablespoons olive oil

2 large onions, diced

3 garlic cloves, minced

5 cups chicken stock or broth

1 14.5-oz can diced tomatoes, undrained

2 teaspoon fennel seeds, crushed

1 head escarole

Salt and pepper to taste

1. Rinse the chicken and pat dry with paper towels. Trim chicken of all visible fat, and cut into ½-inch cubes. Rinse the fennel and cut in half lengthwise. Discard core and ribs, and dice bulb into ¾-inch pieces. Place the chicken and fennel in the slow cooker.

2. Heat olive oil in a medium skillet over medium-high heat. Add onions and garlic and cook, stirring frequently, until onions are translucent, about 3 minutes. Scrape mixture into slow cooker.

3. Stir stock, tomatoes (with juice), and fennel seeds into the slow cooker and stir to combine all ingredients. Cover and cook on Low for 5 to 7 hours or on High for 2½ to 3 hours, or until chicken is cooked through and tender. While soup cooks, rinse escarole. Cut in half, discard core, and cut the remaining escarole into 1-inch strips.

4. If cooking on Low, raise the heat to High. Add escarole to the slow cooker and cook for an additional 30 to 40 minutes, or until the escarole is wilted. Season to taste with salt and pepper, and serve hot.

Fresh fennel, *finocchio* in Italian, and sometimes called *anise* in supermarkets, has a slightly licorice taste but the texture of celery—both raw and cooked. You can always substitute 2 celery ribs for each ½ fennel bulb specified in a recipe.

Spanish Seafood Stew

This is a heartier fish soup than most because it contains both smoky bacon and spicy chorizo sausage. I also love the nuances of orange in the broth.

Makes 4 to 6 servings.

½ lb thick cod fillet

½ lb swordfish fillet

½ lb bay scallops

2 juice oranges, washed

¼ lb bacon, cut into 1-inch pieces

1 medium onion, diced

1 carrot, sliced

1 celery rib, sliced

3 garlic cloves, minced

½ lb chorizo sausage, diced

1 14.5-oz can diced tomatoes, undrained

3½ cups seafood stock or fish broth

3 tablespoons chopped fresh basil

2 tablespoons chopped fresh parsley

1 tablespoon fresh thyme

1 bay leaf

Salt and pepper to taste

1. Rinse fish and pat dry with paper towels. Remove and discard any skin or bones. Cut fish into 1-inch cubes. Refrigerate fish and scallops until ready to use, covered with plastic wrap.

2. Grate off orange zest, and then squeeze oranges for juice. Set aside.

3. Cook bacon in a heavy skillet over medium-high heat for 5 to 7 minutes, or until crisp. Remove bacon from the pan with a slotted spoon, and transfer it to the slow cooker. Discard all but 2 tablespoons of the bacon grease.

4. Add onions, carrot, celery, and garlic to the skillet and cook, stirring frequently, for about 3 minutes or until the onion is translucent. And the chorizo and cook for about 2 minutes more. Scrape mixture into the slow cooker.

5. Add tomatoes (with juice), orange zest, orange juice, stock, basil, parsley, thyme, and bay leaf to the slow cooker. Stir to combine. Cover and cook on Low for 6 to 8 hours or on High for 3 to 4 hours, or until vegetables are soft.

6. If cooking on Low, raise the heat to High. Add the fish and cook for another 30 to 50 minutes, or until it is cooked through and flakes easily. Remove and discard bay leaf. Season with salt and pepper, and serve.

Chorizo is a pork sausage flavored with the Spanish spice *pimenton*, which is similar to paprika, and which gives it the characteristic dark red color. Depending on the type of *pimenton* used, the sausage is spicy or sweet, just as the more common Italian sausages are in the supermarket. Spicy chorizo is most commonly found in the United States and is best in this recipe.

Mmmm-Meatball Soup

The seasoning in the meatballs infuses the broth of the soup during cooking. The result is mm-mm-good!

Makes 4 to 6 servings.

1 lb ground turkey

½ onion, grated

1 carrot, grated

½ teaspoon dried thyme

¼ cup fresh parsley, chopped fine

1 large egg, lightly beaten

10 cups chicken stock or broth

4 cups Swiss chard, coarsely chopped

4 cups kale, coarsely chopped

Salt and pepper to taste

1. In a large bowl, combine ground turkey with onion, carrot, thyme, parsley, and egg. Wash your hands, and mix all the ingredients together with your hands (it's the best way—honestly!). Form meat mixture into meatballs and set aside.

2. Put the chicken broth in the slow cooker and carefully add the meatballs. Cover and cook on Low for 2 to 3 hours or on High for 1 to 2 hours, or until meatballs are cooked through.

3. If cooking on Low, increase the heat to High. Add the chopped chard and kale, cover, and cook an additional 30 to 40 minutes or until greens are soft. Season with salt and pepper.

The chard and kale are hearty greens. You can substitute spinach or collard greens, or do any combination of the greens that you'd like. If you choose to add just spinach, reduce the final cooking time to about 20 minutes, as spinach cooks faster than the others.

Lamb and Carrot Stew

The two main ingredients in this hearty stew are ones you should be able to find at a late spring/early summer farmer's market to capitalize on the freshness of the meat and the vegetables. It's easy to prepare and freezes well, too.

Makes 6 to 8 servings.

4 lbs boneless leg of lamb

1 onion, minced

3 cloves garlic, minced

4 medium carrots, sliced

1 bulb fennel, cored and sliced into thin strips

1 tablespoon cumin

1 tablespoon coriander

1 teaspoon cayenne pepper

1 teaspoon cinnamon

2 tablespoons fresh ginger, grated

½ cup chicken broth or water

1. Trim excess fat off of the lamb, leaving some to flavor the meat and contribute to the sauce. Cut the meat into large chunks. Put it in the slow cooker.

2. Sprinkle the onion and garlic over the meat, then add the carrots and fennel. In a small bowl, combine the cumin, coriander, cayenne, and cinnamon, and stir to mix thoroughly. Add the ginger, then pour the spice mixture over the meat. Top with the broth or water.

3. Cover and cook on Low for 7 to 8 hours or on High for 4 to 5 hours.

Variation:

∗ Substitute 6 pounds of a tougher cut, like shoulder, neck, shanks, or breast for the more tender and less fatty leg of lamb. Don't add the water or broth, as the fat will render to make a lovely sauce.

Sweet Potato and Apple Soup

A vegetable and a fruit synonymous with fall make an amazing, warming soup.

Makes 10 servings.

1 tablespoon ghee
1 large onion, chopped
2 lbs sweet potatoes, peeled and cubed
½ lb carrots, peeled and cubed
2 apples, peeled, cored, and cubed
3 cups chicken broth
1 cup water
Fresh thyme for garnish

1. Heat the ghee in a skillet and add the onion, cooking over medium-high heat until translucent, about 3 to 5 minutes.

2. Into the slow cooker, put the sweet potatoes, carrots, and apples, then stir in the cooked onions. Add the chicken broth and water, stir again, cover and cook on Low for 4 to 5 hours or on High for 2 to 2½ hours until veggies are soft and cooked through.

3. Puree with an immersion blender or in batches in a food processor or blender. Serve hot and garnish with a sprig of thyme if desired.

Variations:

* While this combination of ingredients is always a home run, you can play around with the flavors and textures in this soup by varying the ingredients somewhat. Consider substituting parsnips for the sweet potatoes, and pears for the apples. This will give you creamy pale-colored soup, too, which is beautiful garnished with fresh chives.

Pumpkin and Pear Soup

Another soup made from classic fall foods that is a winner any time you make it.

Makes 6 servings.

2 tablespoons olive oil

1 large onion, chopped

2 lbs pumpkin (or butternut squash) peeled, seeded, and cut into 2-inch pieces

2 Bosc pears, peeled, cored and cubed

4 carrots, peeled and cut into thin slices

6 cups chicken broth

Sprigs of fresh thyme

6 fresh sage leaves

Salt to taste

1. Heat the oil in a skillet and add the onions, cooking over medium-high heat until translucent, about 3 to 5 minutes.

2. Combine the pumpkin, pears, and carrots in the slow cooker. Stir in the chicken broth. Add the cooked onions and stir. Put 3 thyme sprigs on top. Cover and cook on Low for 4 to 5 hours or on High for 2 to 3 hours or until vegetables and fruit are cooked through and soft. Remove the thyme sprigs.

3. Puree with an immersion blender or in batches in a food processor or blender. Season to taste with salt. Serve hot. Garnish with the sage leaves and some additional thyme if desired.

Get festive and serve this soup in a pumpkin shell. All you need to do is cut off the top one-third to make a bowl, and scoop out the seeds and "goop." Place the shell on an oiled cookie sheet at 350 degrees F for about 1 hour, until soft. The pumpkin should be cooked but firm enough to hold the soup inside.

Back-for-More Beef Stew

Slow-cooked beef stew is such a treat. There's something about what happens to the vegetables when the fat and juices from the beef cook for hours alongside them that makes magic from these simple ingredients.

Makes 4 to 6 servings.

2 tablespoons olive oil

1 onion, chopped fine

2 cloves garlic, minced

3 to 4 lbs chuck or bottom round beef

4 carrots, sliced

½ lb green beans, tops and bottoms snipped, and cut into 2-inch pieces

1 turnip, peeled and cubed

4 cups beef stock or broth

1 teaspoon arrowroot for thickener, if desired

1. Heat the oil in a skillet and add the onions and garlic, cooking over medium-high heat until the onion is translucent, about 3 to 5 minutes.

2. Put the beef in the slow cooker and cover with the onion/garlic mixture. Add carrots, beans, and turnips, and pour beef broth over everything.

3. Cover and cook on Low for 6 to 8 hours or on High for 4 to 5 hours. If you like a thicker sauce, when the stew is cooked, take out about a half cup of the juices and mix in the arrowroot. Pour back into the stew and stir to combine. Let sit for 10 to 15 minutes on warm before serving.

If you're in a real hurry, you can make this recipe with frozen vegetables, using traditional carrots, beans, and pearl onions, and also experimenting with some of the vegetable blends (so long as they don't contain corn or peas).

Manhattan Clam Chowder

This tomato-based version of chowder has as many devoted fans as the creamy version has in New England. The combination of the vegetables and herbs in the base makes this recipe a real winner.

Makes 6 to 8 servings.

2 pints fresh minced clams

2 tablespoons olive oil

1 large onion, minced

2 celery ribs, diced

1 carrot, finely chopped

½ green bell pepper, seeds and ribs removed, chopped

1 large turnip, peeled and cubed

1 28-oz can crushed tomatoes, undrained

2 8-oz bottles clam juice

3 tablespoons chopped fresh parsley

1 tablespoon fresh thyme (½ teaspoon dried)

2 teaspoon fresh oregano (½ teaspoon dried)

2 bay leaves

Salt and pepper to taste

1. Drain clams, reserving juice. Refrigerate clams until ready to use.

2. Heat oil in a medium skillet over medium heat. Add onion, celery, carrot, and green pepper. Cook, stirring frequently, for about 5 minutes, or until onion is translucent. Scrape mixture into the slow cooker.

3. Add turnips, tomatoes (and juice), bottled clam juice, juice drained from clams, parsley, thyme, oregano, and bay leaves to the slow cooker, and stir well. Cook on Low for 5 to 7 hours or on High for 2 to 3 hours, or until turnips are almost tender.

4. If cooking on Low, raise the heat to High. Add clams, and continue cooking for an additional 20 to 40 minutes, or until clams are cooked through. Remove and discard bay leaves, season to taste with salt and pepper, and serve hot.

It's now possible to find fresh minced clams in just about every supermarket. If they're not in the refrigerated case, check the freezer. Of course, the fresher the better, and if you can shop for your clams at a fish market or farmer's market, do so. Avoid canned clams.

Watercress Soup

If you like the tangy yet delicate flavor of watercress, you will love this soup, which is thickened with tofu.

Makes 10 servings.

1 cup washed and shredded cabbage leaves

2 bunches watercress, washed, dried, and some stalk removed

1 small zucchini, cut into small pieces

2 large Portobello mushrooms, washed, patted dry, and chopped

8 cups vegetable or chicken broth

4 cups water

4 tablespoons arrowroot, dissolved in 4 tablespoons water to make a paste

2 scallions, white part only, sliced thin

1. Into the slow cooker, add the cabbage, watercress, zucchini, mushrooms, broth, and water. Cover and cook on Low for 3 to 4 hours or on High for 1 to 2 hours.

2. When liquid is bubbly and mushrooms are cooked through, stir in the arrowroot paste and continue stirring with slow cooker on high for a minute or so until thoroughly blended.

3. Stir in the scallions and serve hot.

Those who love watercress love it and wouldn't want to use anything else to make this special soup. There is a distinct pungency to watercress, and that is what makes it so tasty and unique. Arugula is somewhat similar to it, and you could use one-half arugula and one-half baby spinach for the amount of watercress required. Or you could try substituting mustard greens.

Curried Carrot Soup

If you can find high-quality Madras curry, it has a deeper flavor and a bit less heat than standard ground curry powder.

Makes 6 to 8 servings.

2 tablespoons olive oil

2 medium onions, chopped

4 teaspoon curry powder

1 tablespoon fresh ginger, grated

3 lbs carrots, peeled and chopped

4 cups vegetable or chicken broth

5 cups water

Salt and pepper to taste

1. Heat the oil in a skillet and add the onions, cooking over medium-high heat until the onion is translucent, about 3 to 5 minutes. Turn the heat to low and add the curry powder and ginger, stirring constantly for about a minute.

2. Put the carrots in the slow cooker, and scrape the onion mixture in on top. Cover with the broth and water.

3. Cook on Low for 4 to 5 hours or on High for 2 to 3 hours. Use an immersion blender to puree the soup, or process by batches in a blender. Season with salt and pepper, to taste. Serve hot.

Variations:

✳ Substitute butternut squash, pumpkin, or even acorn squash for the carrots in this recipe, and if you want to add some additional spice, add 1 teaspoon cayenne pepper.

Oh, So Satisfying Shrimp and Vegetable Soup

This is a fun soup to make. It's a playful combination of vegetables and shrimp, with a nice dollop of dill.

Makes 4 servings.

2 carrots, peeled and sliced thin

2 cups sugar snap peas, fresh or frozen

2 cups cauliflower florets, cubed

½ lb green beans, trimmed and cut into ½-inch pieces

4 cups chicken broth

4 oz fresh baby spinach, stems removed, washed, and dried thoroughly

2 large egg yolks

½ lb small shrimp, shelled and deveined

2 teaspoon salt

2 tablespoons fresh dill, chopped (optional)

1. Into the slow cooker, add the carrots, snap peas, cauliflower, green beans, and broth. Cover and cook on High for 2 hours.

2. Open the slow cooker and add the spinach, reduce heat to Low, and cook another hour.

3. In a small bowl, whisk the egg yolks until pale. Open the slow cooker and remove about 1 cup of the vegetable mixture into a measuring cup. Add gradually to the egg so that the hot mixture thickens. When thoroughly mixed, put this blend into the slow cooker with the rest, and stir to combine. With the broth heated but not boiling, add the shrimp. Cover and cook until the shrimp are pink and just firm.

4. Season to taste with salt, and serve, garnishing with dill if desired.

> Although peas are a legume and are off the Paleo diet, their relatives that are more pod than pea are acceptable. These include sugar snap peas, snow peas, and green beans.

Spring Sorrel Soup

Sorrel is actually a large herb but is harvested as a leafy vegetable. It has a distinct lemon-tart flavor that makes an excellent soup—especially with the addition of the coconut milk.

Makes 4 to 6 servings.

1 tablespoon olive oil

2 cups fresh sorrel, stems removed and coarsely chopped

1 onion, chopped

2 cups chicken broth

1 can coconut milk

Salt and pepper to taste

1. Heat the olive oil in a skillet and add onions, cooking until translucent, about 5 minutes.

2. Put sorrel into the slow cooker, and add the onions, chicken broth, and coconut milk.

3. Cover and cook on Low for 4 to 5 hours or on High for 2 to 3 hours. Serve hot.

You're not likely to find sorrel in the supermarket, but at a good farmer's market you should find it in the spring. It's easy to grow and is common across Europe. It is high in Vitamin C. The characteristic tartness is from the oxalic acid in the leaves, which is more pronounced in larger, older leaves. Younger leaves are great to put in salad.

Sausage and Pepper Stew

Anyone who shares meals with Italians knows that this is a classic combo of ingredients and flavors. Although Paleo dieters can't serve it on a roll, this thick stew is wonderful accompanied by a salad of fresh greens.

Makes 6 to 8 servings.

1 lb sweet Italian sausage

1 lb hot Italian sausage

1 tablespoon clarified butter

1 onion, thinly sliced

2 bell peppers, seeded and chopped

3 cloves garlic, minced

1 14.5-oz can stewed tomatoes

2 cups chicken stock or broth

1 teaspoon fresh oregano, chopped (or ½ teaspoon dried)

1 teaspoon fresh thyme, chopped (or ½ teaspoon dried)

Salt and pepper to taste

1. Cut the sausages into ¼-inch slices. In a large skillet over medium-high heat, cook the sausages, turning frequently, until browned on both sides. Work in batches if all the meat doesn't fit easily. Remove the browned sausage with a slotted spoon and put it in the slow cooker.

2. Add the clarified butter and the onions to the skillet, and sauté for a couple of minutes until just translucent. Add the peppers and garlic, and cook for another 3 to 5 minutes.

3. Scrape the onion-pepper-garlic mixture into the slow cooker. Top with the tomatoes and broth, and sprinkle oregano and thyme on top. Cover and cook on Low for 5 to 6 hours or on High for 2 to 3 hours. Season with salt and pepper.

If you want a spicier dish, use only hot sausage; if you prefer a milder dish, use only sweet sausage. You can also increase the color by using different colored peppers—a combo of green, red, and even orange if you'd like.

Creamed Cauliflower Soup

The nutty flavor of cauliflower shines through in this decadently creamy recipe. If you can find orange cauliflower, it not only has great color but it contains about 25% more Vitamin A.

Makes 4 to 6 servings.

3 tablespoons coconut oil

1 onion, chopped

2 cloves garlic, minced

3 tablespoons coconut flour

1 can coconut milk

2 cups chicken stock or broth

1 head cauliflower, broken up into pieces, tough stem removed

Salt and pepper to taste

1. In a skillet over medium-high heat, place 1 tablespoon coconut oil and add onions and garlic. Cook stirring constantly until onions are translucent, about 5 minutes. Scrape mixture into the slow cooker.

2. Add the remaining 2 tablespoons of coconut oil to the pan, working over medium heat. When melted, add the coconut flour 1 tablespoon at a time, stirring constantly with a wooden spoon to prevent any lumps from forming. When the flour is all added to the oil, you should have a thick paste. Next, stir in the coconut milk a little at a time, also stirring constantly to prevent lumping. When the milk is mixed in, you should have a thick, creamy mixture.

3. Pour this into the slow cooker. Add the stock and stir, and then pour the cauliflower florets into the mix. Cover and cook on Low for 6 to 8 hours or on High for 4 to 5 hours.

4. If desired, puree the soup with an immersion blender or by batches in a blender.

Tomato Soup

Make this soup when tomatoes are at their ripest—late summer—for the ultimate flavor. If you want a creamy soup, add some coconut milk when pureeing the solids.

Makes 4 to 6 servings.

3 tablespoons coconut oil

1 onion, diced

4 lbs ripe tomatoes, seeds removed and chopped

2 cups chicken stock or broth

½ teaspoon lemon juice

½ to ¾ cup coconut milk, if desired

Fresh thyme, oregano, dill or parsley for garnish

1. In a skillet over medium-high heat, add the oil and onion. Cook the onion until translucent, about 5 minutes. Scrape mixture into the slow cooker.

2. Add the tomatoes and stock. Cover and cook on Low for 6 to 8 hours or on high for 4 to 5 hours.

3. Add the lemon juice when the soup is cooked. Puree the soup using an immersion blender. If you want to make the soup creamy, add the coconut milk while you're pureeing it. Garnish with the herb of your choice.

Variations:

This is a simple and straightforward recipe—just the thing to use as a base for getting creative!

* You can make the soup spicy by adding cayenne or even some sliced jalapenos in the cooking process.
* You can give it a Middle Eastern taste by adding cumin or coriander (in which case you'll want to garnish with coriander).
* You can make a hot gazpacho and top with diced pepper, onion, cucumber, and hard-boiled egg.

Borscht

Borscht is a beet-based soup with its origins in Ukraine. It is now popular throughout Eastern Europe, and becoming more popular worldwide—including your home after you try this!

Makes 6 to 8 servings.

2 tablespoons olive oil

1 lb boneless beef chuck, trimmed and cubed

1 large onion, chopped

2 garlic cloves, minced

1 cinnamon stick

½ teaspoon ground allspice

1 14.5-oz can diced tomatoes

2 bunches beets, with tops, trimmed, peeled and coarsely chopped

1 small bulb celery root, peeled and coarsely chopped

1 small head green cabbage, cored and chopped

3 large carrots, peeled and sliced

2 medium parsnips, peeled and cut into small cubes

4 cups water

3½ cups beef stock or broth

1 bay leaf

¼ cup red wine vinegar

⅓ cup fresh dill or parsley, chopped

1. Heat 1 tablespoon of the oil in a large saucepot over medium-high heat. Add half the beef and stir, cooking until browned on all sides. Transfer the meat with a slotted spoon to a plate, add the other tablespoon of oil, and cook the other half of the meat cubes.

2. Reduce the heat to medium and add the onion, cooking until tender, about 8 minutes. Add garlic, cinnamon stick, and allspice and stir together over heat for about 30 seconds. Add tomatoes with the juice and allow to cook for about 5 minutes, stirring to loosen the browned bits in the pan.

3. Put the meat in the slow cooker and cover with the tomato mixture. Add beets, celery root, cabbage, carrots, parsnips, water, broth, and bay leaf. Stir to combine everything. Cover and cook on Low for 8 to 10 hours or on High for 6 to 7 hours. The beef should be very tender.

4. Remove cinnamon stick and bay leaf. Add vinegar. Sprinkle with dill or parsley when serving.

Borscht (or *borsch*) is the Slavic word for beets. The soup is of Ukranian origin and was always a mildly tart soup that featured root vegetables that could be easily preserved in the cold—beets, onions, turnips, carrots, and potatoes. The featured meat could be beef, pork, chicken, or a combination. The tartness comes from the addition of cabbage and vinegar. While traditionally served with a dollop of sour cream, this isn't necessary to enjoy its richness.

Chapter 6

Paleo Prime Cuts:

Beef, Pork, Lamb, and Game

While our Paleo ancestors no doubt bagged some birds for consumption in their day, it was the larger game, like bison or water buffalo or antelope that made for the choicest feasts around their fires. For us modern Paleos, the same is true. Chicken, turkey, and other fowl make for very tasty meals, but it's the cuts from beef, lamb, pork, and other large(r) game animals that we consider "prime" cuts.

One of the things we thought was important in putting this cookbook together was not to neglect recipes using organ and game meats. While we modern Paleos don't find these on our plates often—or for some maybe never!—our ancestors considered the organs some of the very best pieces of the animal they harvested. Nutrient-dense, the organs were often reserved for community and family leaders and elders. You may not want to make the recipes for liver and onions or Moroccan heart stew before more mouth-wateringly familiar ones such as pot roast, smoked pork, or roast leg of lamb. But you should definitely try them. They may become your favorites after all!

One consideration in regard to selection of meats and cuts: Try to choose the healthiest meats possible. Talk to the meat vendors at farmers' markets, or check the sourcing of meats at a local health food store. The most economical way to keep a supply of meat that has been raised with the health of the animal and those who will feed on it in mind is to buy the whole animal. This is easier with lamb or pork; typically beef is sold in sides or halves. Let the farmer know you are interested in the organs and, in some cases, the tail, the feet, and so on. If there's a cooking method to render these cuts tasty, it's the slow cooker, no question.

Pork Ribs and Apples

What a wonderful combination! These two pair perfectly, and this dish brings them together in a way that's easy to prepare.

Makes 4 to 6 servings.

1 tablespoon coconut oil

2 cloves garlic, sliced thin

2-3 lbs pork ribs

4 large apples, cored and cut into chunks

1 leek, white and pale green part

½ teaspoon cinnamon

½ teaspoon cumin

½ teaspoon cayenne

Salt and pepper to taste

1 tablespoon maple syrup

1. Put the coconut oil and garlic slices in a large skillet over medium-high heat, and cook the garlic for about a minute. Put the pork pieces in and brown on all sides. Transfer the pork to the slow cooker.

2. Put the apples and leeks in the skillet. Stirring frequently, cook for about 5 minutes, until leeks begin to wilt. Add the cinnamon, cumin, cayenne, and some salt and pepper, and stir to coat the apples and leeks. Add the maple syrup and stir again. Scrape the mixture into the slow cooker to cover the pork.

3. Cook on Low for 5 to 6 hours or on High for 2 to 3 hours, until pork is cooked through. Season with additional salt and pepper if desired.

There's no need to peel the apples for this recipe. In fact, leaving the skin on helps the pieces keep their shape. They almost look like potatoes when the dish is cooked. Using large apples reduces the time it takes to core and chop the fruit, but you can use smaller apples if they are what you have. Just increase the quantity.

Pistachio-Crusted Lamb

If you want crunchy pistachios and lamb on the rare side, cook the chops under the broiler. But if you want flavors that slow-cook together for a juicy finish, make it in the slow cooker.

Makes 2 to 4 servings.

1 cup unsalted shelled pistachios, finely chopped

2 tablespoons honey

1 tablespoon fresh lemon juice

1 teaspoon ground cumin

¼ teaspoon cayenne

1½ lbs lamb rib chops

2 tablespoons olive oil

Salt and pepper to taste

1. Put the finely chopped pistachios in a wide-brimmed soup dish. In another dish like this, mix the honey and lemon juice, and in a third, combine the cumin and cayenne. The chops will be dipped in all of these on their way to the slow cooker.

2. Brush the chops with the olive oil, dip and flip in the cumin/cayenne blend, and season with some salt and pepper. In a skillet over medium-high heat, brown the chops on both sides, about 5 minutes a side. When browned, dip both sides of the chop in the honey/lemon combo, and then in the pistachios.

3. Position the chops in the slow cooker. Cook on Low for about 3 hours or on High for about 2 hours so the meat isn't overdone.

These chops are yummy dipped in a cilantro-mint sauce. Make it by combining ½ cup chopped fresh cilantro with ¼ cup chopped fresh mint, 2 tablespoons rice wine vinegar, 2 tablespoons lime juice, and a pinch of salt. Mash these together in a bowl, cover with plastic wrap, and let it sit for at least an hour.

Venison Stew

This is the kind of rich and delicious meal you want to make on a long winter's night. Use some of the cuts that are a bit tougher and therefore benefit most from the long slow-cooking time. These include the shoulder, the shank, and the hindquarters.

Makes 6 to 8 servings.

4-pound venison shoulder

Salt and pepper to taste

4 to 6 slices bacon

¼ cup bacon drippings

2 onions, diced

1 carrot, peeled and diced

1 stalk celery, diced

¼ cup almond flour

1 12-oz can diced tomatoes

½ cup mushrooms, sliced

2 cloves garlic, crushed

3 cups beef stock or broth

1 cup red wine

1 sprig fresh thyme

1 sprig fresh rosemary

2 bay leaves

1. Season the venison with salt and pepper. In a heavy-bottomed skillet, cook the bacon, reserving the cooked strips. In the bacon drippings, cook the venison so that it is browned on all sides. Put the venison in the slow cooker.

2. Into the skillet add the onions, carrots, and celery, and stir frequently until they have browned slightly. Add the almond flour and stir to combine. Put the mixture into the slow cooker with the venison.

3. In a large bowl, combine the tomatoes, mushrooms, garlic, beef stock, red wine, thyme, rosemary, and bay leaves. Pour this over and around the venison.

4. Cook on Low for 6 to 8 hours or on High for 5 to 7 hours.

Eating venison (the meat of deer, but also antelope, elk, and reindeer) and other game meats is a true Paleo experience—though we're lucky to have the herbs and spices we are used to seasoning it with and which we now take for granted. Venison is rich in B vitamins, iron, and phosphorous but low in fat and cholesterol.

Magical Marrow Bones

Our Paleo ancestors would be sure to eat all the marrow from the bones of the animals they killed for food, and we should, too. Here is a recipe for easy beef marrow bones.

Serves 4 to 6.

3 or 4 large beef bones with lots of marrow

Salt and pepper to taste

Put the bones in the slow cooker so the part that you would scoop the marrow out from is facing up. Cook on Low for about 2 hours or on High for about 1 hour. When the marrow is melting and hot, it's ready. Scoop it out of the bones and enjoy it right then and there, with a sprinkle of salt and freshly ground black pepper.

Bone marrow is fat, but it is monounsaturated fat, so it's all good fat. It is also rich in protein, iron, and calcium. While it is rare to find someone 50 years old or younger in the United States who has eaten bone marrow, it is not uncommon for older people, particularly of European descent, to have had it. If you're a fan of the crisp, fatty part of foods like bacon, ribs, and chops, you should enjoy these very much. Be sure to purchase them from a farmer of grass-fed beef, who can also cut them for you.

Oxtail Stew

This is another powerhouse of a Paleo meal, full of the rich goodness of fatty meat and fall vegetables. Start it the day before you're planning to serve it, as you'll need time to separate some of the cooked fat from the dish.

Serves 6 to 8.

2 to 3 lbs beef oxtail
½ cup almond flour
Salt and pepper
3 tablespoons olive oil
1 cup carrots, sliced
1 cup leeks, white part only, sliced thin
4 cloves garlic, minced
½ cup mushrooms, sliced
½ cup parsnips, peeled and cubed
1 cup red wine
2 cups chicken or vegetable stock or broth
2 bay leaves
1 sprig thyme
¼ teaspoons sage
Fresh parsley, chopped, for garnish

1. Put the oxtail pieces in a large bowl, and sprinkle the almond flour, salt, and pepper over them. Turn and shake the pieces to cover with flour. Shake off excess.

2. Heat the oil in a large, heavy bottomed skillet. Remove the oxtail pieces from the flour one by one, shaking to remove excess flour, and put them in the skillet so that all sides are browned. As they're finished, transfer the oxtails to the slow cooker. Remove pan from heat.

3. Add carrots, leeks, garlic, mushrooms, parsnips, red wine, stock, bay leaves, thyme, and sage to the slow cooker. Cover and cook on Low for 8 to 10 hours or on High for about 6 hours, finishing with an hour at Low. After cooking time, turn the slow cooker off and allow everything to cool. There will be a lot of fat in the liquid. With a slotted spoon, transfer the solids to a large serving dish. Cover and refrigerate.

4. Pour the liquid into a bowl and refrigerate it for several hours or overnight, until the fat solidifies. Scoop it out and discard it.

5. The slow-cooked meat and vegetables will be quite soft when you go to reheat them. If desired, add additional vegetables that are just cooked—carrots, green beans, or leafy greens like kale or spinach—and stir them in as the meat is reheating. Heat the stock separately and serve as gravy on the side. Garnish with fresh parsley.

> Oxtail is literally the tail of the ox—or cow. When the animal is butchered, the tail is cut off and skinned, and the bony, muscular tail is cut into segments. It is considered "offal," like other odd parts, and is prepared different ways in different cultures. It is an excellent bone from which to make stock, too.

Stew with Acorn Squash

For this tasty stew, you can use beef or veal—or even turkey breast or cuts of game meat. The acorn squash gives a great color and flavor.

Makes 4 to 6 servings.

½ cup almond flour

¼ cup olive oil

2 lbs stew meat, beef or veal, fat trimmed, cut into 1-inch cubes

1 onion, diced

2 cloves garlic, minced

1 cup red wine

½ cup chicken stock or broth

1 1-lb acorn squash, peeled, seeded, and cut into cubes

2 tablespoons fresh parsley, chopped

2 teaspoons fresh thyme

Salt and pepper to taste

1. Put almond flour in a large bowl and add meat, stirring to coat.

2. Heat oil in a large skillet and add meat pieces, shaking off excess flour as you transfer them from the bowl to the skillet. Brown the meat on all sides. Use a slotted spoon to put browned pieces in the slow cooker.

3. Add onion and garlic to the skillet and cook, stirring, for about 3 minutes. Scrape this onto the meat in the slow cooker.

4. Add wine and stock to the skillet and bring to a boil, dislodging the browned bits in the pan. Pour mixture into the slow cooker. Add squash, parsley, and thyme to the slow cooker, and stir well.

5. Cook on Low for 6 to 8 hours or on High for 3 to 4 hours, or until meat is tender. Season to taste with salt and pepper.

Along with tomatoes and potatoes, squash is a recent addition to European cuisines and came from the New World. Squash seeds have been found in ancient Mexican archaeological digs dating back to somewhere between 9000 and 4000 BCE. The first European settlers originally thought squash to be a type of melon since they had never seen them before.

Short Ribs of Beef with Rosemary and Fennel

Short ribs are a wonderful cut because they become so meltingly tender when slowly braised in the slow cooker. The aromatic rosemary in the simple sauce cuts through the richness of the meat well.

Makes 4 to 6 servings.

5 lbs meaty short ribs with bones

¼ cup olive oil

1 large onion, minced

4 cloves garlic, sliced

2 cups beef stock or broth

1 large fennel bulb, cored, trimmed, and sliced

2 tablespoons fresh parsley, chopped

2 tablespoons fresh rosemary

2 teaspoons arrowroot

Salt and pepper to taste

1. Preheat the oven broiler, and line a broiler pan with heavy-duty aluminum foil. Broil short ribs for 3 to 4 minutes per side, or until browned. Arrange short ribs in the slow cooker, and pour in any juices that have collected in the pan.

2. Heat oil in a medium skillet over medium-high heat. Add onion and garlic, and cook, stirring frequently, for 3 minutes, or until onion is translucent. Scrape mixture into the slow cooker. Add stock, fennel, parsley, and rosemary to the slow cooker, and stir well.

3. Cook on Low for 8 to 10 hours or on High for 4 to 5 hours, or until short ribs are very tender. Remove as much grease as possible from the slow cooker with a soup ladle.

4. If cooking on Low, raise the heat to High. Mix arrowroot with 2 tablespoons cold water in a small cup. Stir this mixture into the slow cooker, and cook on High for 15 to 20 minutes, or until juices are bubbling and slightly thickened. Season with salt and pepper.

Our English word for beef comes from the Latin *bos*, which means "ox." By the Middle Ages, it had become *boef*, or *beef* in English. There were cattle at the Jamestown settlement in Virginia in the early seventeenth century, but the Texas longhorns that we use for beef today were brought to that state by the Spanish almost a century after the Jamestown settlement.

Beef Stew with Paprika

Paprika adds a wonderful smokiness to this dish that is Hungarian in origin.

Makes 4 to 6 servings.

½ cup almond flour

3 tablespoons olive oil

2 lbs stew meat, fat trimmed and cut into cubes

1 large onion, diced

3 cloves garlic, minced

2 tablespoons sweet paprika

2 teaspoons ground cumin

1 cup dry red wine

1 cup beef stock or broth

1 14.5-oz can diced tomatoes, undrained

2 tablespoons fresh parsley, chopped

2 tablespoons fresh rosemary, chopped

1 bay leaf

Salt and pepper to taste

1. Put almond flour in a large bowl and add meat, stirring to coat.

2. Heat oil in a large skillet and add meat pieces, shaking off excess flour as you transfer them from the bowl to the skillet. Brown the meat on all sides. Use a slotted spoon to put browned pieces in the slow cooker.

3. Add onion and garlic to the skillet and cook, stirring, for about 3 minutes. Add paprika and cumin and cook for 1 minute, stirring constantly. Scrape this onto the meat in the slow cooker.

4. Add wine to the skillet, and bring to a boil, stirring to dislodge the brown bits in the skillet. Pour mixture into the slow cooker.

5. Add stock, tomatoes, parsley, rosemary, and bay leaf to the slow cooker, and stir well. Cook on Low for 8 to 10 hours or on High for 4 to 5 hours, or until beef is tender. Remove and discard bay leaf. Season with salt and pepper.

> An easy way to coat food with flour is to place the flour and food in a heavy plastic bag. Keep the air in the bag so the food can move around freely, and hold the top tightly closed with your hand. Shake the food around, and it will be evenly coated.

Steak and Kidney Stew

This is an age-old meat combo that is traditionally the filling for a pie—a great way to use as many parts of the animals as possible, assorted vegetables, and a simple lard-based crust. But there's no need for the "pie" part to enjoy the earthy goodness of this dish.

Makes 6 to 8 servings.

½ cup almond flour

1 teaspoon salt

¼ teaspoon black pepper

2 tablespoons olive oil

1½ lbs beef chuck roast, cut into chunks

1 onion, chopped

3 cloves garlic, minced

½ teaspoon hot paprika

¾ cup beef stock

2 tablespoons tomato paste

1 pair lamb's kidneys, sliced

2 bay leaves

3 carrots, peeled and sliced

2 stalks celery, sliced

1 cup mushrooms, sliced

Salt and pepper to taste

2 tablespoons fresh parsley, chopped

1. Put almond flour, salt, and pepper in a large bowl and add meat, stirring to coat.

2. Heat oil in a large skillet and add meat pieces, shaking off excess flour seasoning as you transfer them from the bowl to the skillet. Brown the meat on all sides. Use a slotted spoon to put browned pieces in the slow cooker.

3. Add onion and garlic to the skillet and cook, stirring, for about 3 minutes. Add paprika and cook for 1 minute, stirring constantly. Scrape this onto the meat in the slow cooker.

4. Add stock to the skillet, and bring to a boil, stirring to dislodge the brown bits in the skillet. Add the tomato paste to combine, and pour mixture into the slow cooker.

5. Cut the kidneys into slices approximately ¼-inch thick, and put them in the slow cooker along with the bay leaves, carrots, celery, and mushrooms. Stir everything together.

6. Cover and cook on Low for 8 to 10 hours or on High for 5 to 7 hours. Remove and discard bay leaves. Season with salt and pepper, and garnish with fresh parsley when serving.

One of the foundations of the Paleo lifestyle is that food source is critically important. Meats should be as "clean" as possible, sourced from farmers who raise them fed on grass. This is especially important when it comes to cooking the offal—parts such as kidneys, livers, sweetbreads, and tripe.

Lamb Shanks with Olives and Artichoke Hearts

While "white meats" are frequently cooked in red wine, it's unusual for red meats to be cooked in white wine. But that's the basis of this dish, punctuated by salty black olives and delicate artichoke hearts.

Makes 4 to 6 servings.

4 to 6 (12- to 14-oz) lamb shanks

3 tablespoons olive oil

1 large onion, chopped

3 cloves garlic, minced

1 cup beef stock or broth

2 ripe tomatoes, seeded and chopped, with juice, or 1 8-oz can tomato sauce

1 cup dry white wine

2 tablespoons fresh rosemary, chopped

2 tablespoons fresh parsley, chopped

12 baby artichokes, trimmed with outer leaves removed, and halved

½ cup pitted black oil-cured olives

1 tablespoons arrowroot

Salt and pepper to taste

1. Preheat the oven broiler, and line a broiler pan with heavy-duty aluminum foil. Broil lamb shanks for 3 minutes per side, or until browned. Transfer lamb to the slow cooker, and pour in any juices that have collected in the pan.

2. Heat oil in a medium skillet over medium-high heat. Add onion and garlic, and cook, stirring frequently, for 3 minutes, or until onion is translucent. Scrape mixture into the slow cooker. Add stock, tomatoes, wine, rosemary, and parsley to the slow cooker, and stir well.

3. Cook shanks on Low for 6 to 8 hours or on High for 3 to 4 hours, or until lamb is almost tender. Add artichokes and olives to the slow cooker, and cook for 2 hours on Low or 1 hour on High.

4. If cooking on Low, raise the heat to High. Mix arrowroot with 2 tablespoons cold water in a small cup. Add this mixture to the slow cooker, cover, and cook for an additional 10 to 15 minutes, or until the juices are bubbling and slightly thickened. Season with salt and pepper to taste.

Like apples and avocados, artichokes darken when exposed to air. When preparing them, have a bowl of cold water acidulated with lemon juice on the counter. Drop the artichokes into it as you trim the stems and pull off the outer leaves.

Liver and Onions

For all you skeptics who have shunned liver in their lives, try this recipe and see if it changes your mind. The slow cooker is magic for offal—not awful!—meats like this.

Makes 2 to 4 servings.

6 slices bacon

2 lbs beef liver

6 yellow onions, peeled and sliced into ¼-inch wedges

1 cup water

Salt and pepper to taste

1 tablespoons fresh parsley, chopped

1. Cook the bacon in a skillet on medium-high heat, transferring it to a plate covered with paper towels when cooked crisp. In the skillet with the bacon fat, fry the liver to lightly brown it on both sides—about 2 minutes a side.

2. Put the liver in the slow cooker and cover with the onions. Crumble and add the bacon, then top with the water. Cover and cook on Low for 6 to 8 hours. (Don't cook on High.)

3. Season with salt and pepper to taste, and garnish with parsley when serving.

Liver is actually a super-food, loaded with protein, vitamins, and minerals and low in fat. While it is high in cholesterol, its benefits outweigh that one shortcoming, and it's truthfully not eaten frequently enough for that to matter for most people. In some cultures, the liver of fresh-killed game is the "prize" for the hunter who makes the kill, and it is eaten fresh out of the animal as it is butchered. Slow-cooking with delicious onions and smoky bacon is more to our liking.

Liver "Tenders"

These nutrient-dense strips of liver and bacon are delicious when paired with almost any veggies, making for very healthy Paleo meals.

Makes 4 to 6 servings.

½ cup almond flour

½ teaspoon salt

¼ teaspoon pepper

2 lbs beef liver, cut into inch-wide slices

6 to 8 slices bacon

¼ cup beef stock or broth

2 tablespoons balsamic vinegar

1. Put the flour, salt, and pepper in a shallow bowl and stir to combine. Dip the liver slices in the flour and coat all sides. Shake off excess and set aside. Discard remaining flour seasoning.

2. Cook bacon in a skillet over medium-high heat, transferring slices to a plate covered with paper towels when crispy.

3. Place liver slices in the slow cooker, and top each one with bacon, securing with toothpicks. Pour beef stock and balsamic vinegar on and around the slices. Cover and cook on High for 2 to 3 hours until the liver is cooked through.

One thing about liver is that if you overcook it, it gets tough and is not very tasty at all—though your canine companion wouldn't mind! This is a dish you should keep an eye on so the tenders don't get overdone.

Moroccan Heart Stew

The rich spices in this recipe make for an exotic meal. Start this the day before you plan to serve it, as the meat needs to marinate.

Makes 6 to 8 servings.

3 lbs lamb hearts (about 6 small to medium-sized hearts)

1 teaspoons cumin

1 teaspoons coriander

1 teaspoons turmeric

½ teaspoons cinnamon

1 teaspoons fresh grated ginger

½ cup olive oil

2 Tbsp lemon juice

4 cloves garlic, crushed

2 onions, chopped

½ cup dried apricots, finely chopped

4 small sweet potatoes, peeled and cubed

⅓ cup kalamata olives, pitted and sliced

2 cups beef broth or stock

2 bay leaves

Salt and pepper to taste

1. Cut the hearts into large cubes, removing any prominent vessels as you do so. Don't get too hung up on cutting out vessels, as they, too, will tenderize with the cooking time. Put the cubes in a large bowl.

2. In a small bowl, measure out all the cumin, coriander, turmeric, cinnamon, and ginger, and stir them with a fork to combine them thoroughly. Whisk in the olive oil, lemon juice, and garlic. Pour this mixture over the meat in the bowl, stir to coat everything, cover the bowl with plastic wrap, and refrigerate overnight.

3. In the morning, using a large skillet and working in batches, cook the meat cubes over medium-high heat, browning on all sides, about 4 minutes a batch. Transfer cubes with a slotted spoon to the slow cooker. If you need some extra oil between batches, use some from the marinade.

4. When the meat is browned and in the slow cooker, add the onions to the skillet and cook, stirring constantly, until they're caramelized, adding some more oil if the skillet is too dry. Put the onions in with the meat.

5. Add the apricots, sweet potatoes, olives, broth, and bay leaves. Stir to combine. Cover and cook on Low for 7 to 9 hours or on High for 5 to 6 hours. Season with salt and pepper to taste.

Heart is a muscle meat, like a roast, but is higher in protein and many other nutrients, including folate, phosphorus, zinc, and several of the B vitamins. Once you get over the "ick" factor with some of these cuts—and you have a recipe that brings out so many flavors—you can start enjoying these dishes (and save money!).

Perfect Pot Roast

A tender and flavorful roast that is as good on a summer night as it is in the heart of winter—when it's done in the slow cooker!

Serves 4 to 6.

1 2- to 3-lb boneless chuck or rump roast

3 tablespoons olive oil

1 large onion, diced

4 cloves garlic, minced

2 cups beef stock or broth

4 ribs celery, trimmed and cut into slices

3 carrots, sliced

2 tablespoons fresh rosemary, chopped

2 tablespoons fresh parsley, chopped

1 teaspoons fresh thyme, chopped

1½ tablespoons arrowroot

Salt and pepper to taste

1. Preheat the oven broiler, and line a broiler pan with heavy-duty aluminum foil. Broil beef for 3 to 4 minutes per side, or until browned. Transfer beef to the slow cooker, and pour in any juices that have collected in the pan.

2. Heat oil in a medium skillet over medium-high heat. Add onion and garlic and cook, stirring frequently, for 3 minutes, or until onion is translucent. Scrape mixture into the slow cooker.

3. Add stock, celery, carrots, rosemary, parsley, and thyme to the slow cooker, and stir well. Cook on Low for 8 to 10 hours or on High for 4 to 5 hours, or until beef is very tender. Remove as much grease as possible from the slow cooker with a soup ladle.

4. If cooking on Low, raise the heat to High. Mix arrowroot with 2 tablespoons cold water in a small cup, and stir it into the slow cooker. Cook on High for 15 to 20 minutes, or until juices are bubbling and slightly thickened.

5. Remove roast from the slow cooker. Season to taste with salt and pepper. Slice it against the grain into thin slices and serve the vegetables and juices on the side. Garnish with some additional parsley if desired.

While roasted meats need time to "rest" during which the juices are reabsorbed into the fibers of the meat, that is not necessary for braised dishes. The juices from the meat are integrated into the sauce, which then moistens the meat.

Barbecued Smoked Pork

Searing meats over aromatic woods on the grill, and then giving them time in the slow cooker, you can replicate the wonderful heady flavor and falling-apart tenderness of traditional barbecue.

Serves 4 to 6.

1½ cups hickory or mesquite chips
1 2½-lb boneless pork shoulder
2 cloves garlic, crushed
Salt and pepper to taste
1½ cups chicken stock or broth
1 cup Paleo BBQ Sauce (page 16)

1. If using a charcoal grill, soak the chips in water for at least 30 minutes. If using a gas grill, place the dry chips in a 12x18-inch piece of heavy-duty aluminum foil. Bring up the foil on all sides, and roll the ends together to seal the packet. Poke several small holes in the top of the packet.

2. Rub pork with garlic, salt, and pepper. Drain the wood chips, and sprinkle chips on the hot coals, or place packet over preheated grid. Place pork on the grill rack and close the grill's lid, or cover it with a sheet of heavy-duty aluminum foil. Smoke pork for 10 minutes per side, turning it with tongs.

3. Place pork in the slow cooker and add stock. Cook pork for 8 to 10 hours on Low or on High for 4 to 5 hours, or until meat is very tender. Season to taste with salt and pepper.

4. Remove pork from the slow cooker, and slice it against the grain into thin slices. Spoon some pan juices over meat, and pass BBQ sauce separately.

Variation:
* To add some spice to the pork, rub in a hint of cayenne or chipotle when you're rubbing in the garlic, salt, and pepper.

Pork Provençal

This vibrant stew punctuated with olives contains many of the flavors common to dishes from this sunny part of southern France, including red bell peppers and leeks. *Tres bon!*

Serves 4.

1½ lbs boneless pork loin, cut into cubes

4 leeks, white parts only

2 juice oranges, washed

2 tablespoons coconut oil

4 cloves garlic, minced

2 red bell peppers, seeds and ribs removed, and thinly sliced

1 14.5-oz can diced tomatoes, drained

1 cup dry red wine

1 cup chicken stock or broth

¾ cup pitted oil-cured black olives

1 tablespoon herbes de Provence

3 tablespoons fresh parsley, chopped

1 bay leaf

1 tablespoon arrowroot

Salt and pepper to taste

1. Preheat the oven broiler, and line a broiler pan with heavy-duty aluminum foil. Broil pork for 3 minutes per side, or until browned. Transfer cubes to the slow cooker, and pour in any juices that have collected in the pan.

2. Trim leeks, split lengthwise, and slice thinly. Place slices in a colander and rinse well under cold running water, rubbing with your fingers to dislodge all dirt. Shake leeks in the colander. Grate zest from oranges and squeeze juice from oranges. Set aside.

3. Heat oil in a medium skillet over medium-high heat. Add leeks, garlic, and red peppers, and cook, stirring frequently, for 3 minutes, or until leeks are translucent. Scrape mixture into the slow cooker.

4. Add tomatoes, orange juice and zest, wine, stock, olives, herbes de Provence, parsley, and bay leaf to the slow cooker, and stir well. Cook on Low for 6 to 8 hours or on High for 3 to 4 hours, or until pork is tender.

5. If cooking on Low, raise the heat to High. Mix arrowroot with 2 tablespoons cold water in a small cup, and stir it into the slow cooker. Cook on High for 15 to 20 minutes, or until juices are bubbling and slightly thickened. Remove and discard bay leaf, and season to taste with salt and pepper.

Pitted olives may be more intention than reality. That's why it's always worth the time to look over pitted olives carefully and not just dump them into a pot. More than one dentist has been called late at night because a patient bit down on an olive to discover a molar-cracking pit.

Lazy Lady's Leg of Lamb

Don't you just love the name of this recipe? You'll love the dish even more—promise! It's so delicious, and always comes out just right, with no fuss!

Serves 6 to 8.

1 tablespoon olive oil

1 bone-in leg of lamb (shank removed)

½ teaspoon sea salt

½ teaspoon freshly ground black pepper

1 teaspoon fresh rosemary, chopped

1 teaspoon fresh mint, chopped

3 cloves garlic, minced

1. Put the olive oil in your hands and rub the oil all over the lamb.

2. Put the lamb in the slow cooker and sprinkle it all over with the salt, pepper, rosemary, mint, and garlic, rubbing the spices onto the meat.

3. Cover and cook on Low for 6 to 8 hours. (Do not cook on High.)

4. Season with additional salt and pepper if desired.

> Serve with a delicious Mint Sauce (page 19) to take this oh-so-easy meal over the top.

Pork Vindaloo

It's all about spicy for me, and this recipe hits the spot.

Makes 4 to 6 servings.

2 tablespoons coconut oil

4 onions, sliced thin

6 chilies, such as jalapenos, habaneros, or a combination, seeded and sliced (wear gloves to do this)

1 teaspoon turmeric

1 teaspoon ground coriander

1½ teaspoons garam masala

½ teaspoons cinnamon

2½ lbs pork butt, trimmed and cut into cubes

2 tablespoons apple cider vinegar

2 tablespoons fresh ginger, grated

10 cloves garlic, peeled

1 teaspoons dry mustard powder

1 14.5-oz can diced tomatoes, undrained

1. Heat oil in a skillet over medium-high heat and add slices of 2 onions. Cook, stirring frequently, for about 3 minutes, until onions are translucent. Add chilies, turmeric, coriander, garam masala, and cinnamon, stirring constantly to coat the onions and chilies with the spices. Remove from heat.

2. Put pork chunks into the slow cooker, and add the onion-spice mixture. Add the garlic cloves, dry mustard, and tomatoes, and stir well.

3. Place the slices from the remaining 2 onions over the pork mixture. Cover and cook on Low for 6 to 8 hours or on High for 4 to 5 hours.

> The whole cloves of garlic in this recipe are a treat to eat. The garlic gets soft and loses its bite and is instead infused with the other spices.

Chapter 7

Paleo-Inspired Poultry

(and Other Fowl)

*W*e had some fun with this chapter, too, looking to include some meats you might not have tried before, like Cornish hen and duck. Slow cooking is an almost fail-safe way to prepare things you might not have considered otherwise. Depending on where you live, you may also have access to fresh Canada goose, which hunters claim bragging rights over for recipes they create.

This chapter is also loaded with more traditional selections, like good ol' roast chicken, which is guaranteed to be juicy and tender when it's prepared in the slow cooker. As in the other chapters, you'll find with the more traditional chicken and turkey recipes that it's really up to what you like and what you have in your pantry that will determine what ends up on your table. You can add all kinds of vegetables, play with different spices, add greater or lesser quantities of liquids for sauce, and so on. The slow cooker has a way of making magic of nearly everything.

All good food starts with the finest ingredients, and sourcing poultry that is raised in the healthiest way will ensure that you not only have an excellent meal but that the nutritive benefits are the best possible, as well. Find a farmer who raises chickens and other fowl, and ask what those birds eat and where they live. Shop at farmers' markets. And don't forget to ask about the organs and other parts that might otherwise be discarded. They are worth slow-cooking!

Country Captain

Country Captain is a chicken dish that dates back to Colonial times. Some food historians say it originated in Savannah, Georgia, a major port for the spice trade. Other sources say a British captain brought the curry-flavored dish flecked with dried currants back from India.

Makes 4 to 6 servings.

6 chicken pieces, 3 each breast and thigh, skin removed

3 tablespoons coconut oil

1 large onion, diced

3 cloves garlic, minced

1 red bell pepper, seeds and ribs removed, diced

1 tablespoon curry powder

½ teaspoon ground ginger

¼ teaspoon freshly grated nutmeg

½ teaspoon dried thyme

⅔ cup dried currants

1 14.5-oz can diced tomatoes, undrained

⅔ cup chicken stock or broth

1 tablespoon arrowroot

Salt and pepper to taste

1. Rinse chicken and pat dry with paper towels. Preheat the oven broiler, and line a broiler pan with heavy-duty aluminum foil. Broil chicken pieces for 3 minutes per side, or until browned.

2. Heat oil in a medium skillet over medium-high heat. Add onion, garlic, and red bell pepper. Cook, stirring frequently, for 3 minutes, or until onion is translucent and pepper begins to soften. Reduce the heat to low, and stir in curry powder, ginger, nutmeg, and thyme. Cook for 1 minute, stirring constantly. Scrape mixture into the slow cooker.

3. Add currants, tomatoes, and stock to the cooker, and stir well. Arrange chicken pieces in the slow cooker, and cook on Low for 6 to 8 hours or on High for 3 to 4 hours, or until chicken is cooked through, tender, and no longer pink.

4. If cooking on Low, raise the heat to High. Mix arrowroot with 2 tablespoons cold water in a small cup. Stir mixture into the slow cooker, and cook for an additional 10 to 20 minutes, or until the liquid is bubbling and has slightly thickened. Season to taste with salt and pepper.

While this dish is associated with the southern United States, it was introduced to the country via New York and Philadelphia as an Indian dish. Famous enthusiasts of the dish include Franklin Delano Roosevelt and General George Patton. As a result of Patton's love of the dish, it is part of the U.S. Army's Ready-to-Eat Field Rations.

Chicken with Spring Vegetables

Chicken is inherently delicate, and that quality is conveyed beautifully in this light dish with accents of pearl onion, asparagus, and even Bibb lettuce.

Makes 4 to 6 servings.

6 chicken thighs, skin removed

2 cups chicken stock or broth

3 tablespoons fresh parsley, chopped

1 tablespoon fresh thyme

1 tablespoon fresh rosemary, chopped

1 tablespoon fresh tarragon

1 bay leaf

2 cloves garlic, minced

1 10-oz package frozen pearl onions, thawed

6 stalks asparagus, tough bottoms removed, cut into ½-inch pieces

2 heads Bibb lettuce, trimmed and cut into quarters

Salt and pepper to taste

1. Rinse chicken and pat dry with paper towels. Preheat the oven broiler, and line a broiler pan with heavy-duty aluminum foil. Broil chicken pieces for 3 minutes per side, or until browned.

2. Add stock, parsley, thyme, rosemary, tarragon, bay leaf, garlic, pearl onions, and asparagus pieces to the cooker, and stir well. Arrange chicken pieces in the slow cooker, and cook on Low for 5 to 7 hours or on High for 2 to 3 hours, or until chicken is almost cooked through.

3. If cooking on Low, raise the heat to High. Add lettuce, and cook for another 30 minutes, or until lettuce is wilted, chicken is tender, and mixture is bubbling. Remove and discard bay leaf, and season to taste with salt and pepper.

> Other spring vegetables you could add include a handful or so of young dandelion leaves or ramps (add with the lettuce).

Indonesian Chicken Curry

This form of curry became very popular in the Netherlands in the nineteenth century because they had substantial land holdings in the part of Southeast Asia that is now Indonesia. It is a fairly mild curry, and the coconut milk makes it appear creamy.

Makes 4 to 6 servings.

1½ lbs boneless, skinless chicken breasts

1 tablespoon Asian sesame oil

2 tablespoons grated fresh ginger

3 scallions, white parts and 4 inches of green tops, chopped

3 cloves garlic, minced

2 tablespoons curry powder

1 teaspoon ground cumin

1 carrot, sliced on the diagonal

½ red bell pepper, seeds and ribs removed, cut into 1-inch squares

1 cup chicken broth or stock

1 cup coconut milk

2 tablespoons rice wine vinegar

2 tablespoons honey

1 tablespoon coconut aminos

1 cup bok choy, sliced

2 ripe plum tomatoes, cored, seeded, and cut into sixths

1½ tablespoons arrowroot

Salt and pepper to taste

1. Rinse chicken and pat dry with paper towels. Cut chicken into 1-inch cubes.

2. Melt oil in a skillet over medium-high heat. Add ginger, scallions, and garlic, and cook, stirring frequently, for 30 seconds, or until fragrant. Reduce the heat to low, and stir in curry powder and cumin. Cook for 1 minute, stirring constantly. Scrape mixture into slow cooker.

3. Add chicken, carrot, red bell pepper, stock, coconut milk, vinegar, honey, and aminos to the slow cooker, and stir well. Cook on Low for 3 to 5 hours or on High for about 2 hours, or until chicken is cooked through. Add bok choy and tomatoes, and cook for 1 more hour on Low or 30 minutes on High, or until bok choy is crisp-tender.

4. If cooking on Low, raise the heat to High. Mix arrowroot with 2 tablespoons cold water in a small cup. Stir mixture into the slow cooker, and cook for an additional 15 to 20 minutes, or until the liquid is bubbling and has slightly thickened. Season to taste with salt and pepper.

> Frequently, coconut milk separates in the can with the liquid on the bottom and a thick layer of coconut on the top. Whisk it briskly until the lumps are gone because they will not break up well with the low heat in the slow cooker.

Everyday Turkey Breast

You might find yourself preparing this at the end of every week so you can slice into it as your week gets busy. It makes a lovely, finished meat that can be used to top salads, roll in lettuce leaves, or even eat out of the fridge.

Serves 6 to 8.

1 4-lb boneless, skinless turkey breast

½ teaspoons salt

¼ teaspoons pepper

1 tablespoons fresh rosemary, chopped

1 tablespoons fresh parsley, chopped

½ cup chicken stock or broth

1. Place the turkey in the slow cooker. Sprinkle with salt and pepper, and add rosemary, parsley, and stock.

2. Cover and cook on Low for 7 to 9 hours or on High for 4 to 6 hours, or until the meat is cooked through.

For easy-to-make, healthy, and delicious snacks, put cut cooked turkey onto a Romaine lettuce leaf, and top with avocado slices, tomato slices, slivered almonds, and diced red onion. Roll the filling up in the leaf and enjoy.

Chicken with Mushrooms

Cacciatore is Italian for "hunter's style," and since Italians in all regions are hunters, this dish is almost a national one. Though several meats can be featured in a cacciatore, they all include tomatoes, onions, pancetta, and mushrooms.

Makes 4 to 6 servings.

6 chicken pieces, skin removed

¼ cup olive oil

2 large onions, halved and thinly sliced

2 cloves garlic, minced

1 lb cremini mushrooms, wiped with a damp paper towel, trimmed, and sliced

1 28-oz can diced tomatoes, undrained

½ cup dry white wine

1 tablespoon fresh thyme

1 tablespoon fresh sage, chopped

1 tablespoon fresh rosemary, chopped

Salt and pepper to taste

1. Rinse chicken and pat dry with paper towels. Preheat the oven broiler, and line a broiler pan with heavy-duty aluminum foil. Broil chicken pieces for 3 minutes per side, or until browned. Transfer pieces to the slow cooker.

2. Heat oil in a large skillet over medium-high heat. Add onions, garlic, and mushrooms and cook, stirring frequently, for 5 minutes, or until mushrooms begin to soften. Scrape mixture into the slow cooker.

3. Add tomatoes, wine, thyme, sage, and rosemary to the cooker, and stir well. Cook on Low for 6 to 8 hours or on High for 3 to 4 hours, or until chicken is cooked through, tender, and no longer pink. Season to taste with salt and pepper.

> Most mushrooms we find in supermarkets are the same species, *Agaricus bisporus*. What makes the difference is their age. White button mushrooms are the youngest, cremini are in the middle, and Portobello is what we call them when they're big and old.

Chicken with Peppers and Olives

Both oranges and olives grow all over Sicily, and those are joined by colorful bell peppers in this exuberant dish that will have you thinking you're vacationing in *la bella Italia!*

Makes 4 to 6 servings.

6 chicken pieces, skin removed

¼ cup olive oil

1 large onions, diced

2 cloves garlic, minced

1 green bell pepper, seeds and ribs removed, diced

1 red bell pepper, seeds and ribs removed, diced

½ cup freshly squeezed orange juice

½ cup chicken stock or broth

½ cup dry white wine

1 14.5-oz can diced tomatoes, undrained

2 tablespoons fresh parsley, chopped

1 tablespoon fresh thyme

1 tablespoon fresh rosemary, chopped

1 tablespoon grated orange zest

2 bay leaves

½ cup pitted oil-cured black olives

Salt and pepper to taste

1. Rinse chicken and pat dry with paper towels. Preheat the oven broiler, and line a broiler pan with heavy-duty aluminum foil. Broil chicken pieces for 3 minutes per side, or until browned. Transfer pieces to the slow cooker.

2. Heat oil in a large skillet over medium-high heat. Add onions, garlic, green pepper, and red pepper. Cook, stirring frequently, for 5 minutes, or until onion is translucent. Scrape mixture into the slow cooker.

3. Add orange juice, stock, wine, tomatoes, parsley, thyme, rosemary, orange zest, bay leaves, and olives to the cooker, and stir well. Cook on Low for 6 to 8 hours or on High for 3 to 4 hours, or until chicken is cooked through, tender, and no longer pink. Remove and discard bay leaves. Season to taste with salt and pepper.

Crispy skin doesn't happen when you're cooking chicken in the slow cooker. That's just a fact. While the chicken is browned for all of these recipes so that the skin looks appealing and not pasty white, if you want crisp skin, place the pieces under the oven broiler, about 8 inches beneath the element, for 3 to 5 minutes, and the skin will become crisp.

Cornish Hens with Fresh Greens

Cornish hens are as easy to make as dishes with chicken pieces, but there's something about them that makes the meal seem extra-special.

Makes 4 to 6 servings.

2 tablespoons olive oil

1 small onion, minced

1 garlic clove, minced

2 small Cornish game hens, split in two, skin removed

1 head Swiss chard, washed, coarse stems removed, and leaves chopped in large pieces

1 head Escarole, washed, trimmed, and chopped in large pieces

½ cup chicken stock or broth

1 lb baby spinach leaves

Salt and pepper to taste

1. Heat oil in a small skillet over medium-high heat, and cook onions and garlic about 3 minutes, or until onion is translucent. Scrape mixture into slow cooker.

2. Place Cornish hens on top of onion mixture, and top with Swiss chard, Escarole, and broth.

3. Cover the slow cooker and cook on Low for 6 to 7 hours or on High for 3 to 4 hours, or until chicken is tender and cooked through. Add the baby spinach and cook for another 20 to 30 minutes. Season with salt and pepper.

The Cornish Game hen is a young, immature chicken, which is technically not supposed to be over 5 weeks of age or more than 2 pounds. It's the result of crossing the Cornish Game and Plymouth or White Rock chicken breeds. You probably won't find these at farmers' markets, so they won't be as fresh as free-range birds. But they are impressive and a nice change of pace.

Super-Tender Chicken

This dish can be served as-is with various vegetable side dishes, or additional vegetables can be added to it to make a stew or thick soup.

Makes 4 to 6 servings.

½ cup almond flour

Salt and pepper

8 chicken thighs, skin removed

2 tablespoons coconut oil

1 onion, diced

1 cup dry white wine

1 cup chicken stock

1 teaspoon fresh tarragon

1 cup coconut milk

Salt and pepper to taste

1. Put almond flour, salt, and pepper in a shallow bowl and whisk to combine. Dip chicken thighs into flour, turning to coat, and shake off excess flour and set aside.

2. Heat oil in a large skillet, and add the chicken pieces. Brown the chicken on both sides, about 3 minutes a side. Transfer browned pieces to the slow cooker. Add the onion and, if necessary, some additional oil, and cook the onion for about 3 minutes, until translucent. Sprinkle a tablespoon or two of almond flour on the onions and stir to coat.

3. Add wine to the pan and stir, dislodging browned bits. Add chicken stock and bring continue to cook, stirring, while liquid thickens, about 10 minutes. Add tarragon, and pour liquid onto the chicken.

4. Cover and cook on Low for 5 to 6 hours or on High for 3 to 4 hours. Add the coconut milk and cook an additional 15 to 30 minutes until the liquid is bubbling. Season with additional salt and pepper.

The primary herb in this recipe is tarragon. It is a French herb that has long, fine leaves. It has a mild flavor of anise, or licorice, though it is distinctly different. An essential ingredient of bearnaise sauce in France, it is used to season chicken, egg, and fish dishes as well. It is a strong flavor, so a little goes a long way.

Turkey Kabobs

This is fun food for the kids—and the adults! Vary the vegetables you use depending on what's super-fresh.

Makes 4 to 6 servings.

⅓ cup olive oil

1 tablespoons herbes de Provence

2 cloves garlic, mashed

¼ teaspoon salt

½ teaspoon pepper

1 4-lb boneless, skinless turkey breast, cut into cubes

1 red bell pepper, seeded and cut into large chunks

1 green bell pepper, seeded and cut into large chunks

1 onion, cut into thick wedges

1 zucchini, cut into thin slices

2 quarts ripe cherry tomatoes

Wooden skewers, cut or broken into sizes to fit into the slow cooker

1. In a large bowl, combine the olive oil, herbes de Provence, garlic, salt, and pepper, and stir to combine. Add the turkey, red and green peppers, onions, and zucchini, and toss to coat all.

2. Put the turkey and vegetables onto the skewers, working in the cherry tomatoes. Put the skewers in the slow cooker as you finish them. Pour the remaining dressing over the skewers.

3. Cook on Low for 3 to 4 hours or on High for 2 to 3 hours until fish is cooked through and vegetables are crisp-tender.

Variation:

✳ Spice it up by adding some cayenne to the dressing or by including slices of fresh seeded, sliced jalapenos or other hot peppers.

> Before you start skewering turkey and veggies, be sure your wooden skewers are short enough—or cut or broken—to fit into the slow cooker.

Duck Confit

Once you taste how good this is, you'll be eager to serve your lovely confit to family and friends. You can serve it in many ways, from "as is"—the just-cooked legs themselves—to shredded over salads, over sautéed greens, or just for delicious snacking. You can use the fat for roasting winter vegetables or other meats.

Serves 6.

¼ cup kosher salt

1 tablespoon freshly ground black pepper

8 fresh thyme sprigs, leaves stripped off for use

3 bay leaves

2 teaspoons juniper berries

6 whole duck legs

2½ lbs duck fat (this will yield about 5 cups)

1. In a small bowl, combine the salt, pepper, thyme leaves, bay leaves, and juniper berries. Rinse the duck legs with cold water and pat dry with paper towels. Place in a large baking dish and spread the salt rub evenly on all sides. Cover and refrigerate overnight to cure the meat.

2. When ready to cook the legs, place the duck fat in the slow cooker and put the heat on High to melt the fat. Remove the duck legs from the refrigerator and, one at a time, take them out of the pan and rinse them under cold water. Pat them dry with paper towels. When the fat is melted, add the legs to the cooker.

The fat should stay at a simmer, so you'll want to turn the heat down to Low. Cover and cook on Low for about 4 hours. When cooked, the meat will be very tender and fall away from the bones.

3. Remove the cooked legs immediately, eating them right away or allowing them to cool for later use.

4. Put the fat from the slow cooker into a glass bowl that can fit the legs back into it and that can be securely sealed. When the fat and legs have cooled, put the legs into the bowl and refrigerate. The duck confit is good this way in the fridge for about 6 months. When ready to use, just remove a leg and allow it to come to room temperature so the fat can melt before using or eating.

In essence, this is a simple dish of cured duck legs preserved in fat. It is considered a luxury, however, because it tends to be time-consuming and most people aren't sure what to do with it once it's prepared. Here is a great, easy recipe. You will need to purchase the duck legs and fat at a specialty butcher or grocery store, but once you have the fat, you can reuse it. It also requires marinating overnight.

Duck with Apples and Currants

This is a fabulous fall dish since it is loaded with apples. The currants add a hint of sweetness and pair really well with the duck.

Makes 4 to 6 servings.

2 lbs fresh duck parts, skin on

8 firm, fresh baking apples, cored and cut into cubes, but not peeled

3 cloves garlic, minced

2 tablespoons dried currants

¼ teaspoon cinnamon

½ teaspoon salt

1 cup red wine

1. Rinse the duck and pat dry with paper towels. Put it in the slow cooker.

2. Add the apples, garlic, currants, cinnamon, salt, and wine, and stir to combine.

3. Cover and cook on Low for 6 to 8 hours, or on High for 4 to 5 hours, or until meat is very tender.

Variation:

✶ Turn the apple mixture into a cream sauce by adding ½ cup coconut milk into it and bringing it to a slow boil so that it blends.

Turkey Meatballs and Squash

A family favorite—and you might even get some help forming the meatballs.

Serves 6 to 8.

1 lb ground turkey

1 egg

½ onion, minced

1 tablespoons fresh parsley, chopped fine

2 cloves garlic, put through a garlic press

Salt and pepper to taste

2 large zucchini, sliced thin

1 14.5-oz can diced tomatoes, undrained

1. In a large bowl, combine the turkey, egg, onion, parsley, garlic, and a sprinkling of salt and pepper. Stir thoroughly.

2. Put the zucchini slices in the slow cooker. Form the meat into meatballs, and put them on top of the zucchini. Add the tomatoes over everything.

3. Cover and cook on Low for 4 to 6 hours or on High for 3 to 4 hours, until meatballs are cooked through and zucchini is tender. Season with additional salt and pepper if desired.

Variations:

* Substitute any other kind of ground meat in this recipe. With the egg, onion, parsley, and garlic, you'll still fashion delicious meatballs. Vary the spices to create different flavor profiles.

Wild Goose a l'Orange

This is for everyone with friends or family who hunt game birds. The breasts of wild geese are lean and delicious if cooked properly. There is little to no fat, so it's important not to overcook the meat.

Makes 2 to 4 servings.

¼ cup bacon or duck fat (or olive oil)

2 whole breasts, halved, skin removed

½ teaspoon salt

¼ teaspoon pepper

2 small oranges, peeled, seeded, and segments halved

1 apple, cored and cubed

1 onion, cut into small wedges

1 6-oz can frozen orange juice concentrate, thawed

1. Heat fat in slow cooker on Low. Add goose breasts, flesh side down. Sprinkle with salt and pepper. Add orange segments, apple, onion, and orange concentrate. Cover and cook on Low for 6 to 8 hours, checking the meat to be sure it isn't overcooked but that it is tender.

2. When ready to serve, remove breasts, discarding fruit and onions. Season with additional salt and pepper.

Although you won't be using the fruit sauce that the bird has cooked in as a gravy when serving, you can make a delicious ginger glaze for the meat. In a small saucepan, combine 1 tablespoon freshly grated ginger, 1 tablespoon fresh chopped cilantro, 2 tablespoons honey, and about ½ cup water. Stir and bring to a boil, then remove from heat. Pour onto the meat or serve on the side.

Chapter 8

Paleo by the Sea and Stream

*I*f eating a Paleo diet is your path to eating more fresh fish, then it can be well worth it. Fresh fish—and by this we mean wild-caught fish—is loaded with beneficial Omega-3 fatty acids and is a great source of protein. Fish prepared in the slow cooker comes out moist and delicious, with little of its nutritive value depleted by cooking.

The debate over farm-raised versus wild-caught fish is significant for those following the Paleo plan. Since the idea is to cleanse your system of the impurities in our over-processed food chain, it's important to consider the source of your fish, just as it is for meat and poultry. The reports on farm-raised fish verify the use of antibiotics and other medications, as well as color-enhancing compounds, and more. One of the best sources we've found for assistance in this tricky process is the Monterey Bay Aquarium Seafood Watch, at www.montereybayaquarium.org. The Seafood Watch has seafood ratings that list top choices, good alternatives, and what to avoid. Check it out!

The recipes in this chapter range from simple and elegant—like salmon on a bed of spinach and garlic—to complex and creative, like the hearty seafood stew. Fish is delicious any night of the week, so indulge!

Fish with Tomatoes and Fennel

In this colorful dish, fish fillets are cooked on top of an aromatic bed of vegetables scented with orange. Close your eyes and pretend you're dining on the Italian coast.

Makes 4 to 6 servings.

2 medium fennel bulbs

¼ cup olive oil

1 large onion, thinly sliced

2 cloves garlic, minced

1 28-oz can diced tomatoes, drained

1 tablespoon grated orange zest

½ cup freshly squeezed orange juice

1 tablespoon fennel seeds, crushed

2 lbs thick, firm-fleshed fish fillets (such as cod, halibut, or tilapia), cut into serving-sized pieces

Salt and pepper to taste

1. Discard stalks from fennel, and save for another use. Rinse fennel, cut in half lengthwise, and discard core and top layer of flesh. Slice fennel thinly and set aside.

2. Heat oil in a large skillet over medium-high heat. Add onion and garlic, and cook, stirring frequently, for 3 minutes, or until onion is translucent. Add fennel and cook for an additional 2 minutes. Scrape mixture into the slow cooker.

3. Add tomatoes, zest, orange juice, and fennel seeds to the slow cooker. Stir well to combine. Cook on Low for 5 to 7 hours, or on High for 2 to 3 hours, or until fennel is crisp-tender.

4. If cooking on Low, raise the heat to High. Season fish with salt and pepper, and place it on top of vegetables. Cover and cook for 30 to 45 minutes, or until fish is cooked through and flakes easily. Season to taste with salt and pepper.

The vegetable mixture can be cooked up to 2 days in advance and refrigerated, tightly covered. Reheat it in a microwave oven or over low heat, and return it to the slow cooker. Increase the heat to High and cook the fish just prior to serving, as described above.

Poached Fish with Vegetables and Herbs

This is a southern Italian version of bouillabaisse, in a way, because it combines so many delicious fresh fish paired with fragrant fresh herbs and tomatoes. *Mangia!*

Serves 4 to 6.

1 lb thick, firm-fleshed white fish fillets, such as cod, halibut, or tilapia, cut into serving pieces

¼ cup olive oil, divided

Salt and pepper to taste

1 large Vidalia onion, halved and thinly sliced

2 celery ribs, sliced

½ small fennel bulb, trimmed, cored, and thinly sliced

2 cups fish stock or broth

1 14.5-oz can diced tomatoes, undrained

½ cup fresh parsley, chopped

2 tablespoons fresh oregano, chopped, or 2 teaspoons dried

2 teaspoons grated lemon zest

1 bay leaf

½ lb large shrimp, peeled and deveined

1 dozen littleneck clams, well scrubbed

1. Rinse fish and pat dry with paper towels. Rub fish with 2 tablespoons of olive oil, and sprinkle with salt and pepper. Refrigerate, tightly covered with plastic wrap.

2. Heat oil in a large skillet over medium-high heat. Add onion, celery, and fennel, and cook, stirring frequently, for 3 minutes, or until onion is translucent. Scrape mixture into the slow cooker.

3. Add stock, tomatoes, 3 tablespoons parsley, oregano, lemon zest, and bay leaf to the slow cooker, and stir well. Cook on Low for 4 to 5 hours or on High for 2 to 3 hours, or until vegetables are crisp-tender.

4. If cooking on Low, raise the heat to High. Add fish, shrimp, and clams, and cook for 45 minutes to 1 hour, or until fish is cooked through and flakes easily.

5. Remove and discard bay leaf, and season with salt and pepper. Garnish with parsley when serving.

The laurel tree, native to Asia Minor, from which the bay leaf comes, was very important in both ancient Greece and Rome. The laurel can be found as a central component in many ancient mythologies that glorify the tree as a symbol of honor. In the Elizabethan era, some people believed pinning bay leaves to one's pillow on the eve of St. Valentine's Day would bring the image of your future spouse to your dream.

Monkfish Kabobs

The nice thing about making kabobs in the slow cooker is that you don't have to worry about parts or all of them burning on the grill.

Makes 4 to 6 servings.

⅓ cup olive oil

1 tablespoons herbes de Provence

2 cloves garlic, mashed

¼ teaspoon salt

½ teaspoon pepper

2 lbs monkfish, cut into cubes

1 red bell pepper, seeded and cut into large chunks

1 green bell pepper, seeded and cut into large chunks

1 onion, cut into thick wedges

1 zucchini, cut into thin slices

2 quarts ripe cherry tomatoes

Wooden skewers, cut or broken into sizes to fit into the slow cooker

1. In a large bowl, combine the olive oil, herbes, garlic, salt, and pepper, and stir to combine. Add the fish, red and green peppers, onions, and zucchini, and toss to coat all.

2. Put the fish and vegetables onto the skewers, working in the cherry tomatoes. Put the skewers in the slow cooker as you finish them. Pour the remaining dressing over the skewers.

3. Cook on Low for 3 to 4 hours or on High for 2 to 3 hours until fish is cooked through and vegetables are crisp-tender.

Variation:

* Spice it up by adding some cayenne to the dressing, or by including slices of fresh seeded, sliced jalapenos or other hot peppers.

> Before you start skewering fish and veggies, be sure your wooden skewers are short enough—or cut or broken—to fit into the slow cooker.

Tuna Steaks with Mango Salsa

Super-fresh tuna is amazing with this south-of-the-border salsa. You may want to make a little extra to serve on the side!

Makes 4 to 6 servings.

4 tuna steaks (about 6 oz each), and at least ¾-inch thick

3 tablespoons coconut oil

3 cloves garlic, minced

1 large ripe mango

1 red bell pepper, seeded, cored, and diced

1 medium jalapeno, seeded and diced (use gloves to do this)

1 small red onion, diced

2 tablespoons fresh-squeezed lime juice

Salt to taste

2 tablespoons fresh cilantro, chopped

1. Rub tuna with 1 tablespoon of the oil.

2. Combine remaining oil, garlic, mango, red pepper, jalapeno, onion, lime juice, and a pinch of salt in a small bowl to make the salsa.

3. Place tuna in the slow cooker. Cook on Low for about 1 hour, or on High for about 40 minutes.

4. Turn the steaks gently with a slotted spatula. Put the salsa on the fish, turn the heat to High, and cook for an additional 15 to 20 minutes for rare, or longer for fish that is better done. Sprinkle with cilantro.

If you want to make extra mango salsa, just double or triple the amount of the ingredients used to make it—everything except the fish, really! Add the cilantro to the fresh salsa. Because salsa loses some of its *umph* when it's cooked, I prefer to use it as a garnish instead of adding it in the cooking process with the fish.

Shrimp Creole

The Creole cuisine of Louisiana is an amalgam of French, Italian, and Spanish influences tempered with African-American, and shrimp Creole is one of its premier dishes.

Makes 4 to 6 servings.

3 tablespoons coconut oil

6 scallions, white parts and 3 inches of green tops, chopped

2 celery ribs, sliced

½ green bell pepper, seeded and diced

3 cloves garlic, minced

1 tablespoon dried oregano

1 tablespoon paprika

1 teaspoon ground cumin

½ teaspoon dried basil

1 15-oz can tomato sauce

½ cup fish stock or broth

2 bay leaves

1½ lb extra-large shrimp, peeled and deveined

Salt and cayenne to taste

1. Heat oil in a medium skillet over medium-high heat. Add scallions, celery, bell pepper, and garlic. Cook, stirring frequently, for 3 minutes, or until scallions are translucent. Reduce the heat to low, and stir in oregano, paprika, cumin, and basil. Cook for about 1 minute, stirring constantly. Scrape mixture into the slow cooker.

2. Add tomato sauce, stock, and bay leaves to the slow cooker, and stir well. Cook on Low for 4 to 6 hours or on High for 2 to 3 hours, or until vegetables are soft.

3. If cooking on Low, raise the heat to High. Remove and discard bay leaves, and stir in shrimp. Cook for 15 to 30 minutes, or until shrimp are pink and cooked through. Season to taste with salt and cayenne.

Do not equate the words "fresh shrimp" with shrimp that have never been frozen. The truth is you probably would be unable to find never-frozen shrimp fresh from the ocean unless you net it yourself. That's because these days shrimp are harvested, cleaned, and flash-frozen on the boats before they ever reach the shore. But if you plan to freeze shrimp, ask the fishmonger to sell you some still frozen rather than thawed in the case.

Swordfish with Lemon and Capers

Swordfish is such a wonderfully meaty fish that it stands up to some stronger seasonings, including capers. They add an extra tang to the lemony dish.

Makes 2 to 4 servings.

2 lbs swordfish steaks

2 lemons

Salt and pepper to taste

2 tablespoons capers

2 tablespoons clarified butter

¼ cup fish stock or water

1 tablespoon fresh dill, chopped

1. Put the swordfish steaks on a piece of aluminum foil that will be big enough to wrap over the fish to form a sealed cooking "tent." With the fish in the middle of the piece of foil, squeeze the juice of the lemons over them, removing seeds as you go. Sprinkle the fish with some salt and pepper, then put the capers over it. Cut the butter into small pieces and dot the steaks with it. Bring up the sides of the foil and begin to form the packet.

2. When the sides are up, add the stock or water before securing all edges together and fully enclosing the fish.

3. Put the packet in the slow cooker. Cook on Low for 3 to 4 hours or on High for 2 to 3 hours. It's cooked when the flesh flakes easily but is still moist. Be careful not to overcook.

4. When serving, pour the sauce from the packet over the fish. Garnish with dill.

Variation:
You can substitute almost any meaty fish for the swordfish in this recipe. Try:
* Tuna
* Monkfish
* Mako
* Cod
* Mackerel

Caribbean Curried Fish

Creamy coconut milk tones down the fiery peppers and curry in this delicious stew. Although the recipe calls for grouper, you can also use halibut, tilapia, or even monkfish.

Makes 4 to 6 servings.

2 tablespoons coconut oil

2 medium onions, diced

4 cloves garlic, minced

1 jalapeno or Scotch bonnet pepper, seeds and ribs removed and finely chopped (wear rubber gloves to do this)

2 tablespoons curry powder

1 tablespoons ground cumin

3 ripe plum tomatoes, cored, seeded, and diced

2 14-oz cans coconut milk

1½ lbs grouper or other thick firm-fleshed white fish, rinsed and cut into 1-inch cubes

Salt and pepper to taste

1. Heat oil in a medium skillet over medium-high heat. Add onions, garlic, and pepper. Cook, stirring frequently, for 3 minutes, or until onion is translucent. Reduce the heat to low, and stir in curry powder and cumin. Cook for 1 minute, stirring constantly. Scrape mixture into the slow cooker.

2. Add tomatoes and coconut milk to the slow cooker, and stir well. Cook on Low for 6 to 8 hours or on High for 3 to 4 hours, or until vegetables are soft.

3. If cooking on Low, raise the heat to High and cook for an additional 25 to 35 minutes, or until fish is cooked through and flakes easily. Season with salt and pepper.

Scotch bonnet peppers are some of the hottest in the world. A relative of the habanero pepper, Scotch bonnets are grown and used widely in Jamaican cooking, most notably in their distinctive "jerk" sauces. Much of a pepper's heat is stored in the ribs and seeds of the pepper, in oils in the cells. To avoid getting it on your fingers and then possibly in your eyes or other thin-skinned areas of your body, you should wear rubber gloves to handle and chop the peppers.

Rare Salmon with Salsa Topping

The slight rare finish of this dish leaves the fish succulent and tasty, with the perfect strength of flavor for the fresh "salsa" topping.

Makes 4 to 6 servings.

4 to 6 salmon steaks (about 6 oz each), and at least ¾-inch thick

3 tablespoons coconut oil

3 cloves garlic, minced

2 tablespoons ground cumin

2 tablespoons chili powder

Salt and pepper to taste

4 ripe plum tomatoes, cored, seeded, and chopped

3 scallions, white parts and 3 inches of green tops, chopped

3 tablespoons fresh chives, snipped

2 tablespoons fresh-squeezed lime juice

1. Rub salmon with 1 tablespoon of the oil. Combine garlic, cumin, chili powder, salt, and pepper in a small bowl. Rub mixture on both sides of the salmon.

2. Combine remaining oil with tomatoes, scallions, chives, and lime juice.

3. Place salmon in the slow cooker. Cook on High for about 40 minutes. Turn salmon gently with a slotted spatula. Top salmon with the tomato mixture, and cook on High for an additional 20 to 30 minutes for rare fish, or longer for fish that is more done.

Many of the thick, firm-fleshed fish like salmon, halibut, cod, tilapia, and flounder, can be purchased frozen. It's handy to keep a supply of fish fillets in your freezer. Dethawing them so they don't lose flavor or texture is the secret to successful recipes. We've found the best way is to put individual fillets in plastic baggies with air-tight seals, and then submerse in a bowl of cool (not warm!) water. It only takes about 15 minutes to thaw. Or put the frozen fillets in the refrigerator for several hours.

Bouillabaisse

This one-pot meal of assorted fish and shellfish is bursting with flavor.

Makes 4 to 6 servings.

1 large white onion, chopped

3 cloves garlic, minced

2 large stalks celery, fronds removed, finely chopped

1 red bell pepper, seeded and chopped

8 oz clam juice

½ cup water

2 tablespoons extra virgin olive oil

1 tablespoon lemon zest

1 tablespoon fresh basil, chopped

1 tablespoon fresh parsley, chopped

½ teaspoon onion powder

1 teaspoon fresh oregano

1 teaspoon fresh thyme

1 bay leaf

1 lb thick, firm-fleshed white fish, such as tilapia, cut into 1-inch pieces

¾ lb shrimp, shelled and deveined

½ lb squid, cleaned and sliced

8 oz cleaned, fresh crabmeat

Salt to taste

¼ cup fresh parsley, chopped

1. In a large bowl, combine onions, garlic, celery, red pepper, clam juice, water, olive oil, zest, spices, and bay leaf. Mix well. Put into slow cooker. Cover and cook on Low for 4 to 5 hours or on High for 2 to 3 hours until vegetables are tender.

2. If cooking on Low, increase heat to High. Remove and discard bay leaf. Add fish, shrimp, squid, and crab and cook for an additional 30 to 45 minutes until fish is done. Season with salt and pepper to taste, and garnish with fresh parsley.

This classic French fish "boil" is said to have originated in the seaside town of Marseilles in the south of France. The word itself has a fanciful attribution—*bouille-abbesse*, or the abbess' boil—in reference to a particular Abbesse in a convent there; and the more practical bouillon abaissé, meaning, "to reduce by evaporation."

Zucchini-Ginger Mahi-Mahi

A simple dish, for sure, but you'll find the flavors meld beautifully. The fresh ginger is the key ingredient.

Makes 4 to 6 servings.

4 medium zucchini, sliced into ¼-inch rounds and then cut in half to form half moons

1 tablespoons fresh ginger, grated

2 cloves garlic, minced

2 tablespoons water

3 lbs mahi-mahi, cubed

Salt and pepper to taste

Sprigs of fresh parsley

1. In a large bowl, combine zucchini, ginger, garlic, and water. Stir to combine and add to the slow cooker. Cook on Low for 3 to 4 hours or on High for about 2 hours.

2. If cooking on Low, increase heat to High. Add fish. Cover again and cook an additional 30 to 40 minutes, until fish is cooked through and tender. Season with salt and pepper, and garnish with fresh parsley.

> Mahi-mahi are also called *Dolphinfish*, though they bear no relation to dolphins. They are considered one of the most beautiful fish in the sea, with brightly colored flanks. They can be found worldwide in tropical and subtropical waters. Mahi-mahi is prized for its sweet, mild flavor and large, tender flakes when cooked.

Catfish Gumbo

Gumbo is a fish stew native to Southern Louisiana and featuring okra. The catfish is a flavorful fish; you can substitute something milder like halibut if desired.

Makes 4 servings.

2 tablespoons olive oil

1 small white onion, chopped

2 cloves garlic, minced

2 red bell peppers, seeded and cut into thin strips

1 16-oz can whole tomatoes, undrained and chopped

1½ lbs okra, trimmed, and sliced into ½-inch rounds

1 teaspoons lemon zest

Salt

1 cup water

4 catfish filets, about 5 ounces, boned

Salt, pepper, and cayenne to taste

1. In a large skillet, heat the oil over medium-high heat, add the onion and garlic, and cook, stirring, for about 3 minutes or until onion is translucent. Add the red pepper strips and continue stirring for another minute.

2. Put mixture into slow cooker, and add tomatoes, okra, zest, and salt to taste. Stir to combine, then top with 1 cup of water. Cook on Low for 5 to 6 hours or on High for 3 to 4 hours until peppers are tender.

3. Reduce or keep heat to Low and add the fish filets. Cover and cook an additional hour or so until fish is cooked through and tender. Season with salt and pepper—and a pinch of cayenne if you like it spicy.

This south-of-the-border dish features the ingredient that is synonymous with gumbo: okra. It's a vegetable people tend to love or hate. It's the slimy consistency it can take on that tends to turn people off. To minimize that, bring the okra to room temperature an hour before you will cook with it. After cutting the vegetable into rounds, let it sit an additional 30 to 60 minutes to dry out some more.

Brook Trout with Lemon

This recipe calls for cooking the fish whole, but don't worry—filleting it when it is cooked is easy. It makes an elegant presentation on the plate, and there's something very satisfying about removing the skeleton yourself.

Makes 2 to 4 servings.

2 medium to large whole brook trout, cleaned by the fishmonger but not filleted

2 lemons

2 teaspoons herbes de Provence

Salt to taste

2 tablespoons clarified butter

⅔ cup dry white wine

1 tablespoon fresh parsley, chopped

1. Put 1 trout each on pieces of aluminum foil that are big enough to wrap over the fish to form a sealed cooking "tent." With the trout in the middle of the piece of foil, squeeze the juice of 1 lemon over each, removing seeds as you go. Sprinkle each fish with a teaspoon of herbes de Provence and some salt. Cut the butter into 4 small pieces and place two pats each on top of the fish. If desired, slice the lemons and place 2 slices in the cavity inside each fish.

2. Bring up the sides of the foil and begin to form the packet. When the sides are up, pour 1/3 cup wine on each trout before securing all edges together and fully enclosing the fish.

3. Put the trout packets in the slow cooker. Cook on Low for 2 to 3 hours or on High for 1 to 2 hours. Halfway through, peek into one of the packets to see how the fish is doing. It's cooked when the flesh is pale and easily flakes away from the bones. Make sure it's cooked through before removing from packets and serving. Serve whole, pouring the sauce in the packet over the fish. Garnish with parsley.

Removing the trout's skeleton so your fish is free of bones is easy if you take your time. With the fish on your plate, loosen the flesh close to the spine and gently scrape/slide the top "fillet" off the skeleton. When it's off and half the skeleton is exposed, lift the head or tail of the trout and gently pull back and lift up to pull the remaining skeleton away from the fillet on the bottom. Discard the skeleton.

Salmon with Spinach

This is a great throw-together meal for busy households because you can use frozen salmon fillets. Thaw them by placing each fillet in an air-tight plastic baggie and submersing in a bowl of cool water. It takes about 20 minutes to thaw several fillets at once.

Makes 2 to 4 servings.

4 16-oz bags fresh baby spinach greens (or a spinach/kale combo)

2 cloves garlic, minced

2 tablespoons coconut oil

4 frozen salmon fillets, thawed

Salt to taste

2 tablespoons toasted sesame seeds

1. Working in batches, put spinach in the colander and give it a quick rinse, picking through the leaves and removing any large stems. Shake excess water from the spinach, but don't dry thoroughly. Put spinach in slow cooker after rinsing. When all spinach is in the slow cooker, add the garlic and oil and stir to combine and coat the leaves.

2. Place the salmon fillets on top of the spinach greens. Cook on Low for about 1 hour, until spinach is wilted and fish is cooked through. Depending on how well done you like your salmon, you may want to cook it an additional 15 to 20 minutes.

3. In a small, dry skillet over medium-high heat, add the sesame seeds and cook, shaking lightly or stirring to keep the seeds from sticking and burning, until seeds are lightly toasted, about 2 minutes. Garnish salmon and spinach with the sesame seeds, and season with salt to taste.

One of the reasons for eliminating grain is that it is the cause of inflammation. Frozen fish fillets are usually from farm-raised fish that are grown in pens and often fed with grains. For this reason, people looking to get the most out of their Paleo diet should choose wild-caught over farm-raised fish.

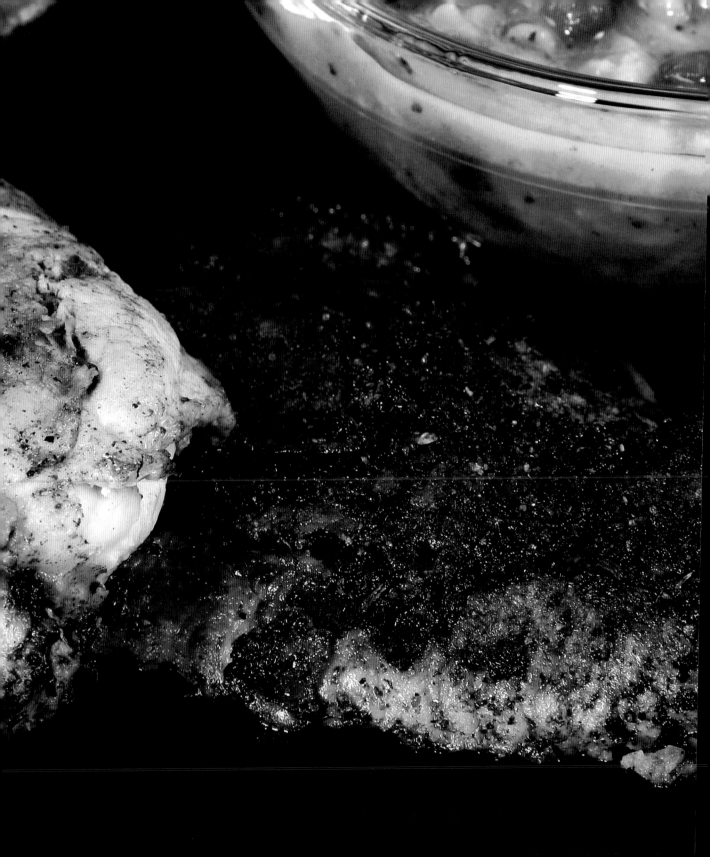

Cajun Catfish

Smoky, spicy, and succulent, this is a fiery dish that is excellent served with a salad of crisp greens, fennel, and citrus.

Makes 2 to 4 servings.

3 lbs catfish fillets

1 tablespoon olive oil

3 tablespoons Cajun seasoning (see sidebar)

1 lemon

¼ cup dry white wine

1. Working with thin rubber gloves on, rub the catfish fillets with some olive oil, and then rub with Cajun seasoning, being sure to coat all sides. Place seasoned fillets in slow cooker and squeeze the juice from the lemon over them, being sure to pick out the seeds. Add the wine.

2. Cook on Low for 1 to 2 hours or on High for about 1 hour until fish is cooked through and flakes easily with a fork.

3. Mix all ingredients thoroughly and store in an airtight glass container.

You can purchase pre-mixed Cajun seasoning, or have fun making your own blend.
The traditional ingredients are:
- 5 tablespoons cayenne pepper
- 3 tablespoons black pepper
- 3 tablespoons onion powder
- 3 tablespoons garlic powder
- 3 tablespoons chili powder
- 1 tablespoon dried thyme
- 1 tablespoon dried sweet basil
- 1 tablespoon salt

Chapter 9

Paleo-Friendly Vegetable Dishes

*I*t would be over-simplistic and misleading to say the Paleo lifestyle centers around meat. There is much more to Paleo—and to life!—than meats. Fresh vegetables are key. Your choices are practically unlimited, and you can eat as many veggies as desired.

The only vegetables you'll need to steer clear of on your Paleo diet are certain legumes, most notably beans, as they are difficult to digest and contain some of the same anti-nutrients as some grains. These include black beans, lentils, chickpeas, green peas, and peanuts (and peanut butter). None of the recipes here contain these vegetables.

Keep a broad and deep supply of fresh vegetables so you can turn to them for snacking any time. When you return from shopping for your vegetables, take the time to prepare them so they are ready to eat when you get hungry. The transition to Paleo—like any transition—is the most challenging part of the change from what you're used to, so make it as easy as possible. Peel and cut up carrots, cucumbers, zucchini, broccoli, celery, fennel, and peppers, and store them in air-tight containers. Make sure you have clean, fresh greens like spinach, lettuce, kale, collards, arugula, and so on. They are the base of any kind of salad you want to make with the other veggies—and they're great to munch on by themselves.

When it comes to slow cooking the vegetables, it'll also be handy to have them cleaned and cut up so that preparation is super-simple. Some vegetables—such as sweet potatoes, turnips, and cabbage—need to cook longer. Others, like tender greens, get added to a slow-cooker recipe in the last 15 minutes or so. Our recipes will lead you through that, step by step.

Asian Butternut Squash

Butternut squash is such a delicious and satisfying vegetable, and in this dish, the addition of orange zest and aromatic Chinese five-spice powder adds complexity to the already earthy taste.

Makes 6 to 8 servings.

1 (2½ pound) butternut squash, peeled and cubed

½ cup fresh-squeezed orange juice

1 tablespoon grated orange zest

1 tablespoon coconut aminos

3 tablespoons coconut oil

¼ teaspoon Chinese five-spice powder

Salt and pepper to taste

1. Place squash in the slow cooker. Combine orange juice, orange zest, aminos, coconut oil, and Chinese spice powder in a small bowl and whisk to combine well. Pour the mixture over the squash.

2. Cook on Low for 5 to 6 hours or on High for 3 to 4 hours, or until squash is tender. For chunky squash, mash cubes with a potato masher right in the slow cooker. For smooth squash, spoon the contents of the slow cooker into a food processor fitted with a steel blade, and puree until smooth using on-and-off pulsing. Season to taste with salt and pepper.

Chinese five-powder spice is available in more and more grocery stores, as well as in Asian specialty stores. It is a combination of cloves, cinnamon, star anise, Szechuan peppercorns, and fennel. It packs a flavor punch, and a little goes a long way, but it does give amazing complexity of flavors.

Sweet Potatoes and Apples

This is a New England version of candied sweet potatoes, with applesauce and maple syrup providing moisture while cinnamon adds a bit of aroma and spice. Serve it with any simple poultry or pork dish, and even with game meats such as venison.

Serves 4 to 6.

1 tablespoon coconut oil (for greasing the slow cooker)

3 large sweet potatoes or yams, peeled and thinly sliced

2 Granny Smith apples, peeled, cored, and thinly sliced

1 cup chunky applesauce

2 tablespoons maple syrup

2 tablespoons coconut crystals

6 tablespoons coconut butter, melted

¼ teaspoon ground cinnamon

Pinch of salt

1. Grease the inside of the slow cooker with coconut oil.

2. Arrange half the sweet potatoes and apples in the slow cooker. Combine applesauce, maple syrup, coconut crystals, melted butter, cinnamon, and salt in a mixing bowl. Pour half the mixture over the sweet potatoes and apples, and repeat with remaining potatoes, apples, and mixture.

3. Cook on Low for 6 to 8 hours or on High for 3 to 4 hours, or until sweet potatoes are tender.

Although sweet potatoes and yams are used interchangeably in recipes, they are different tubers. Yams are native to Africa and have a flesh that is lighter in color but sweeter than sweet potatoes. Yams also have a higher moisture content, so cut back slightly on liquids if you are using an authentic yam in a dish.

Braised Fennel

Fennel has an almost silky texture and sweet flavor once it is braised. This dish is like a utilty infielder in baseball; it goes with almost anything and everything, especially dishes with dark colors and assertive seasonings.

Makes 4 to 6 servings.

2 medium fennel bulbs, about 1 lb each

2 tablespoons coconut butter

½ small onion, thinly sliced

1 clove garlic, minced

1 cup vegetable stock or broth

1 teaspoon fresh thyme, or
¼ teaspoon dried

Salt and pepper to taste

1. Cut stalks off fennel bulb, trim root end, and cut bulb in half through the root. Trim out core, then slice fennel into 1-inch-thick slices across the bulb. Arrange slices in the slow cooker, and repeat with second bulb.

2. Heat coconut butter in a small skillet over medium heat. Add onion and garlic and cook, stirring frequently, for 3 minutes, or until onion is translucent. Scrape mixture into the slow cooker.

3. Add stock and thyme to the slow cooker. Cook on Low for 4 to 6 hours or on High for 2 to 3 hours, or until fennel is tender. Season to taste with salt and pepper.

> Although the celery-like stalks are trimmed off the fennel bulb for this dish, don't throw them out. They add a wonderful anise flavor as well as a crisp texture and are used in place of celery in salads and other raw dishes.

Roasted Beets

If you love beets, you'll love this method of cooking them. It "beats" waiting a long time for them to cook in boiling water!

Serves 6 to 8.

2 bunches beets with tops (about 2 pounds)

2 tablespoons olive oil

1 clove garlic, minced

Greens from the beets, washed and cut into 1-inch pieces

Salt to taste

1. Scrub the beets clean and cut into 1-inch pieces.

2. Heat the oil in a medium skillet over medium-high heat and add the garlic. Cook, stirring constantly, about 1 minute. Add the beet greens and continue cooking and stirring until greens are just wilted, about 3 minutes.

3. Put beets into the slow cooker, topping with the greens. Cover and cook on Low for 4 to 5 hours, or on High for 3 to 4 hours, or until beets are soft. Season with salt and serve.

Betacynin is the pigment that gives red beets their deep color. Some people's bodies aren't able to process betacynin during digestion. As a result, their urine may be colored pink. This is temporary and is in no way harmful.

Artichokes with Lemon and Herbs

Artichokes can be intimidating because they are spiky and can take a long time to cook when steamed. The slow cooker is the perfect way to make great artichokes. Set them in the cooker and come home to perfectly cooked artichokes.

Serves 6 to 8.

4 to 6 artichokes, depending on size of vegetables and the slow cooker

1 lemon, quartered

3 cloves garlic, crushed

1 teaspoon fresh rosemary, minced

2 cups water

1. Wash and pat dry the artichokes. Trim the stem to about ¼ inch from bottom. Pull off the first couple of layers of leaves at the bottom, and snip the pointy ends off the leaves all around the chokes.

2. Place the artichokes in the slow cooker, bottoms down. Squeeze the juice of the lemons over the artichokes and put the squeezed quarters in with the artichokes, distributed throughout. Peel the garlic cloves and crush with the back of a knife. Put the garlic cloves in the slow cooker, distributed throughout. Sprinkle rosemary around the artichokes.

3. Pour 2 cups water around the artichokes so that it covers the bottom of the slow cooker with about ½ to 1 inch of water. Cover and cook on Low for 6 to 8 hours or on High for 4 to 5 hours. Artichokes should be tender, with leaves easily breaking away from the core. Serve hot or at room temperature with the lemon/garlic juice as a dipping sauce for the leaves.

Artichokes are a lot of fun to eat as you work your way through the leaves to what is considered the vegetable's most delicious part, its heart. Peel each leaf off and dip the bottom into the lemon-garlic cooking liquid, or into some melted coconut butter. Put the leaf in your mouth, press down with your teeth, and scrape the tender flesh from the lower part of the leaves. Work through the artichoke until the leaves are small and nearly transparent. Pull off the last tip of leaves. The heart will be left, attached to the stem. There is some "fuzz" on the top of the heart that needs to be gently scraped off, as it can be bitter. It falls off easily. Now enjoy the heart!

Braised Artichokes

Quartering the artichokes decreases the cooking time while still yielding the delicious slow-cooked goodness of the whole choke. The quarters are tender enough to eat whole, without having to peel off the leaves to eat the fleshy parts.

Makes 4 to 6 servings.

2 to 3 large artichokes
2 tablespoons coconut butter
2 cloves garlic, minced
1 lemon, juiced
1½ cups vegetable stock or broth
1 tablespoon fresh parsley, chopped
Salt and pepper to taste

1. Wash and pat dry the artichokes. Trim the stems back, snip off the pointy ends of the leaves, and cut into quarters. Arrange sections in the slow cooker.

2. Heat coconut butter in a small skillet over medium heat and in it cook the garlic until just soft and perfumed, about 2 minutes. Scrape butter and garlic mixture into the slow cooker.

3. Add lemon juice and stock so that it is about ½ to 1 inch deep in the cooker. It should nearly cover the sections. Cover and cook on Low for 4 to 6 hours or on High for 2 to 3 hours, until artichoke sections are tender throughout. Add parsley and cook on Low for another 10 to 15 minutes. Season to taste with salt and pepper.

The artichokes found in the United States are grown in California, though it was Mediterranean European countries where the vegetables originated and have been eaten for centuries. The name comes from the Italian word *articoclos*, which is said to refer to a pine cone. It is part of the thistle family, and plants grow three to six feet tall. The vegetable is the plant's flower bud, harvested before it flowers.

Persian Ratatouille

If you're looking for a variation on the more traditional ratatouille, this is a really good one that pairs especially well with lamb and beef.

Makes 4 to 6 servings.

1 large butternut squash, peeled, seeds removed, and cut into small cubes

1 large eggplant, cubed

4 large tomatoes, seeded and coarsely chopped

2 large carrots, sliced

1 large onion, chopped

4 cloves garlic, minced

1 cup chicken stock or broth

1 teaspoon turmeric

½ teaspoon coriander

½ teaspoon cumin

1 tablespoon tomato paste

Salt and pepper to taste

1. Place the cubed squash in the slow cooker. In a large bowl, combine the eggplant, tomatoes, carrots, onion, and garlic. Stir well to combine. Put the vegetable mix on top of the squash.

2. In the measuring cup with the chicken stock, add the spices and tomato paste, and stir to combine. Pour this over the vegetables. Cover and cook on Low for 3 to 4 hours or on High for about 2 hours, or until vegetables are tender. Season with salt and pepper.

Variation:

* If you want the dish to have some heat, add ½ teaspoon cayenne pepper with the spices.

Glazed Carrots

Adding a hint of something sweet to slow-cooked carrots turns them from tasty to terrific.

Makes 4 to 6 servings.

2 lbs carrots, peeled and cut quartered lengthwise into 4-inch sticks

½ cup vegetable broth or water

1 tablespoon coconut crystals or maple syrup

1 teaspoon olive oil

2 tablespoons fresh parsley or dill, chopped

1. Place carrot sticks in slow cooker. In a small bowl, combine the broth or water, coconut crystals or syrup, and olive oil. Pour the liquid over the carrots.

2. Cover and cook on Low for 2 hours until carrots are tender. Open the lid and keep it propped open with the handle of a wooden spoon, and continue to cook for 20 to 30 minutes until some liquid is cooked off and the carrots glaze. Garnish with fresh parsley or dill before serving.

Carrots could be considered Paleo "candy"—a vegetable that also has a fairly high sugar content. Fortunately, that sugar is naturally occurring and a "treat" in the truest sense of the word. Carrots are loaded with other vitamins and minerals, most notably beta carotene, from which they get their color. The brighter the better!

Stuffed Peppers

By using different-colored bell peppers, make this meal as good to look at as it is to eat.

Makes 4 servings.

2 orange bell peppers
2 red bell peppers
2 tablespoons olive oil
1 onion, chopped
3 cloves garlic, minced
1 lb ground turkey
2 green bell peppers, seeded and chopped
1 cup diced fennel
1 cup sliced domestic mushrooms
2 tablespoons chili powder
½ teaspoon cinnamon
1 teaspoon salt
1 28-oz can diced tomatoes
1 6-oz can tomato paste

1. Working carefully, cut off the tops of the orange and red peppers and remove the seeds from inside. Set aside.

2. In a large skillet over medium-high heat, add the olive oil, onions, and garlic. Cook until onions are translucent, about 3 minutes. Add the ground turkey to the skillet and continue to cook, stirring, until meat is browned, about 5 minutes.

3. Next add the chopped green peppers, fennel, mushrooms, chili powder, cinnamon, and salt, and continue cooking, stirring constantly, until combined and heated through, about 5 minutes.

4. Fill the emptied peppers with the meat mixture, and place the peppers, bottoms down, into the slow cooker one at a time.

5. In a small bowl, combine the diced tomatoes and tomato paste. Add the tomato sauce to the cooker. Cover and cook on Low for 5 to 6 hours or on High for 4 to 5 hours.

Variation:

✳ To add some heat and additional flavor, replace the green bell pepper with some fresh, sliced hot peppers like jalapenos or habaneros.

Kale and Bacon

The bacon does double-duty in this recipe, not only adding crunchy flavor bites once the kale is cooked but providing a fat base in which to prep the greens.

Makes 4 to 6 servings.

6 pieces of bacon, chopped

1 onion, diced

2 lbs curly kale, tough stems removed and coarsely chopped

Salt and pepper to taste

1. Put bacon in a skillet and heat to medium high. Cook bacon pieces until browned and just getting crisp, transferring cooked pieces to a plate covered with a paper towel. Set bacon aside.

2. Put onion in bacon fat and cook, stirring, for about 2 minutes until onion is translucent. Add kale to skillet and cook, stirring, until kale is just coated with bacon fat, about 2 minutes. Transfer kale and onions to the slow cooker. Cook on Low for 2 hours or on High for about 1 hour.

3. When kale is cooked through, transfer to a bowl. Stir in the cooked bacon bits and serve.

Variations:

∗ The kale in this recipe can be substituted for collards, Swiss chard, sorrel, and even full-grown spinach (not baby spinach leaves).

Slow and Stewy Mushrooms

Mushrooms are one of those vegetables that you can slow-cook for nearly forever so long as you keep an eye on the liquid. The longer they cook, the better they taste.

Makes 4 to 6 servings.

2 lbs mushrooms, preferably a mix of button, crimini, and Portobello

¼ cup olive oil

1 cup beef stock or broth

Salt and pepper to taste

1. Clean the mushrooms by wiping away dirt with a soft cloth or mushroom brush. Remove the toughest part of the stems, and slice into thick slices/chunks.

2. Heat the oil over medium heat in a large skillet and add the mushrooms. Stir to coat with the oil and cook, stirring for about 5 minutes.

3. Transfer the mushrooms to the slow cooker, add the beef stock, sprinkle with salt and pepper, and stir to combine. Cover and cook on Low for 7 to 9 hours, or on High for 5 to 6 hours. Stir once during cooking to be sure there is enough liquid, which there should be. For the last 30 minutes of cooking, turn to High and remove the lid. This will cook the mushroom broth down a bit to make the dish slightly thicker.

Slow-cooked mushrooms are often flavored with some vermouth during the last part of the cooking process. While there's no consensus about the Paleo appropriateness of vermouth itself, the fact that it is made from grapes flavored with a blend of herbs, bark, and roots, a dry vermouth seems to meet the requirements. Add a tablespoon to this recipe in the last 30 minutes of cooking time and see what you think.

Curried Vegetables

Set the table with Indian-inspired linens and tableware, because the smell of this dish cooking is going to make you feel like you are far, far away.

Makes 6 to 8 servings.

1 tablespoon coconut oil

1 onion, chopped

2 cloves garlic, minced

6 carrots, sliced

1 head cauliflower, florets only

1 small turnip, peeled and cubed

1 tablespoon fresh ginger, grated

2 tablespoons curry powder

½ teaspoon coriander

½ teaspoon cayenne pepper

½ teaspoon cinnamon

1 cup chicken stock or broth

Salt and pepper to taste

1 tablespoon fresh coriander, chopped, for garnish

1. In a skillet over medium-high heat, melt the coconut oil and add the onion, garlic, and carrots. Cook, stirring, for about 5 minutes. Scrape the mixture into the slow cooker.

2. In a bowl, combine the cauliflower and turnip chunks and mix together. Add the ginger, curry powder, coriander, cayenne, and cinnamon. Stir to combine, and add this to the slow cooker.

3. Cover with the chicken stock, then cook on Low for 4 to 5 hours or on High for 2 to 3 hours. Season with salt and pepper, and garnish with fresh coriander when serving.

> The ginger root is in the same family as turmeric and cardamom—other traditionally Indian spices. Ginger has long been used for many medicinal purposes, most notably indigestion.

Asparagus with Pancetta

These wrapped asparagus are delicious, of course, but also make great snacks. And they're fun to eat.

Makes 6 to 8 servings.

1 lb asparagus

1 lb pancetta, sliced very thin

1 tablespoon clarified butter or ghee, melted

1. Wash and dry asparagus spears, trimming off tough bottoms by about an inch.

2. Wrap each spear in a slice of pancetta, and lay the spears gently and carefully in the slow cooker.

3. Drizzle the spears with the melted butter. Cover and cook on Low for about 2 hours or on High for about 1 hour, until spears are tender. Turn heat to high and cook for an additional 15 to 20 minutes with the lid propped open with the handle of a wooden spoon to allow steam to escape. This will dry-crisp the pancetta somewhat.

> While thin spears are usually more desirable for quick cooking when steaming asparagus, for this recipe it is preferable to select fatter spears so there is more inside the wrap of pancetta.

Garlic Mashed Cauliflower

This super-simple recipe produces such a flavorful and creamy dish that you will not miss traditional mashed potatoes loaded with butter or sour cream. Enjoy!

Makes 6 to 8 servings.

2 14-oz bags of frozen cauliflower florets

Hot water to cover

1 small head of garlic, roasted

1 tablespoon coconut oil

Salt and pepper to taste

1. Put the cauliflower in the slow cooker and add hot tap water until the florets are just covered. Cover and cook on Low for 4 to 5 hours or on High for 2 to 3 hours until cauliflower is tender.

2. **While the cauliflower is cooking in the slow cooker,** roast the garlic. To do this, preheat the oven to 400 degrees F. Peel off the outermost layers of skin on a whole clove of garlic, and cut off about ¼ to ½ inch from the top so the cloves are exposed. Put the head on a baking pan (like a muffin tin or cake pan), and drizzle about a teaspoon of olive oil on the top, being sure to coat it. Cover with aluminum foil and bake for about 30 to 40 minutes. Allow to cool before squeezing out cloves.

3. Drain the cauliflower and put it in a bowl. Add the roasted garlic cloves and the oil, and mash with a potato masher or puree with an immersion blender, mashing to desired consistency. Season with salt and pepper.

Ready-When-You-Are Spaghetti Squash

As this squash is the Paleo-friendly replacement for pasta in a variety of recipes, families with children may be making a lot of it. This is a great way to cook the squash while you're gone for the day, so you can return home, scoop it out, and prepare an easy topping or side dish.

Serves 4 to 6.

1 average-size spaghetti squash (about 4 lbs)

2 cups water

Salt and pepper to taste

1. Pour 2 cups of water into the slow cooker. Wash and dry the outside of the squash, and place it into the slow cooker. Cover and cook on Low for 6 to 8 hours. Remove the squash with tongs and allow to cool for about 20 minutes until it can be safely handled.

2. Cut the squash in half and remove the seeds. Use a fork to scoop/peel out the meat, which naturally falls into spaghetti-like strands. Season with salt and pepper, and if serving as a simple side dish, add a tablespoon of clarified butter.

Spaghetti squash is a winter vegetable that can be stored in a cool, dry place for several months, which is why it's found in some markets year-round. It has a pale ivory skin, and the flesh is rich in beta carotene and other nutrients. It's a high-carb, low-calorie treat.

Brussels Sprouts

Slow cooking this earthy veggie mellows its tanginess but brings out its woodsy depth of flavor. A touch of mustard and a hint of sea salt add the perfect finish.

Makes 4 to 6 servings.

1 lb Brussels sprouts

3 tablespoons olive oil or ghee

1 teaspoon dry mustard

Pinch of sea salt

1. Wash and trim the Brussels sprouts, cutting off the coarsest part of the bottom and a layer or so of the leaves on the bottom. Cut the sprouts in half, and put them in the slow cooker.

2. In a measuring cup, mix the olive oil with the dry mustard. Pour over the Brussels sprouts. Cover and cook on Low for 3 to 4 hours or on High for 2 to 3 hours. Before serving, add a pinch of sea salt.

While mustard adds a wonderful tanginess to this recipe, you can substitute other spices to get different flavors. For spicier sprouts, add some cayenne pepper or Asian chili sauce; for an Indian taste, add curry or cumin.

Roasted Tomatoes

Because the slow cooker retains the moisture in foods, these won't need to cook long to become moist and flavorful. Seasoned with some herbs and garlic, they make a colorful and tasty side dish.

Serves 4 to 6.

4 large, ripe tomatoes, cut in half, seeds removed

2 cloves garlic, minced

1 teaspoon fresh oregano, minced, or ½ teaspoon dried

Salt and pepper to taste

1 teaspoon fresh parsley, chopped

1. Place cut tomatoes bottom down in the slow cooker. Sprinkle minced garlic on top, then sprinkle with the oregano.

2. Cover and cook on Low for 3 to 4 hours or on High for 1 to 2 hours. Season with salt and pepper, and garnish with the parsley.

Summer-ripe tomatoes taste too good to cook—use them in salads, salsas, or to stuff with some meat or vegetable mix. Slow cooking is great for off-season tomatoes, preferably vine-ripened.

Broccoli Rabe

Consider this your "lazy" way to great broccoli rabe. Compile your ingredients, put them in the slow cooker, and come back many hours later to something truly delicious. The longer this slow cooks, the better, and if you put it on warm after 8 hours, it can go a few more hours.

Makes 4 to 6 servings.

1 lb broccoli rabe

6 large cloves garlic, sliced

1 teaspoon red pepper flakes

⅓ cup extra virgin olive oil

Salt to taste

1. Prepare the broccoli rabe by removing the tough stems and setting aside only the tops and the tender parts of the stems. Put these in a colander and rinse, then spin or pat dry.

2. Put the prepared broccoli rabe in the slow cooker and add the garlic, red pepper flakes, and olive oil. Cover and cook on Low for 6 to 8 hours. Do not cook on High. Season with salt to taste.

Broccoli rabe, which has long been popular in Italy and Portugal, is related to broccoli and is a member of the turnip family. It is definitely more bitter than broccoli.

Chapter 10

Paleo Desserts:

Sweet Without Sugar!

*D*id you think you'd have to give up desserts to take up a Paleo diet? Think again! Dark chocolate is a Paleo-approved ingredient! And almond flour, and coconut milk—and eggs, of course!

Fruit is a great sweet treat on its own, and there's nothing like fresh, locally grown, ripe fruit when it is in season. Strawberries. Melons. Blueberries. Apples. They are all so delicious when they're in season at the local market—or in your own garden! The Paleo diet brings a renewed appreciation for how delicious fresh fruit really is. Savor it!

In this chapter, though, we'll go beyond the simple joy of fresh fruit to help you make desserts that will have even non-Paleos coming back for more. Flan, banana bread, even chocolate mousse! So get your slow cooker out and treat yourself every once in a while.

Baked Stuffed Apples

The honey and nuts complement the full flavors of fall in this classic dessert.

Serves 4 to 6.

½ cup chopped walnuts

4 to 6 baking apples, such as Jonathan and Northern Spy

½ cup dried currants

2 tablespoons coconut oil

2 tablespoons honey

1. Preheat the oven to 350 degrees F, and line a baking sheet with parchment paper. Place walnuts on the baking sheet and toast nuts for 5 to 7 minutes, or until browned. Set aside.

2. Core apples and peel the top half only. Arrange apples in the slow cooker. Combine nuts, currants, oil, and honey in a small bowl. Spoon equal portions of mixture into cores of apples.

3. Cook on Low for 4 to 5 hours or on High for 2 to 3 hours, or until apples are tender when pierced with a knife. Serve hot, at room temperature, or chilled.

It's important to peel the top half of the apple. If you don't, the steam builds up inside the skin and the apple tends to fall apart.

BananaRama

I gave this dessert a fun name because it's a fun—and yummy!—dessert, full of the gooey goodness of ripe bananas.

Makes 2 to 4 servings.

4 bananas, very ripe
4 tablespoons coconut butter
1 teaspoon 100% vanilla extract
2 tablespoons honey

1. Peel the bananas and slice them in half length-wise. Place the bananas in the slow cooker. Dot the bananas with the coconut butter.

2. In a small bowl, mix the vanilla and honey. Drizzle over the bananas.

3. Cover and cook on Low for 2 to 3 hours or on High for about an hour. Serve warm.

Use this Paleo dessert as a base upon which to add lots of things, including dried fruits, toasted (unsweetened) coconut, toasted nuts, cinnamon, ginger, or combinations of these and other foods and spices, to your liking.

Baked Pears with Ginger

To get the most flavor from this aromatic and satisfying dish, use pears that are good 'n ripe.

Makes 4 servings.

4 large, ripe pears, cored and cut into chunks or slices

1 teaspoon ground ginger

1 teaspoon lemon zest

2 tablespoons coconut butter, cut into bits

1. Put the pear slices into the slow cooker. Sprinkle with the ginger and the lemon zest. Put bits of coconut butter over the fruit.

2. Cover and cook on Low for 3 to 4 hours or on High for about 2 hours. Serve warm or at room temperature.

Variations:
* Add some crunch to the recipe by topping with toasted nuts—pepitas, sesame seeds, and almonds are all good choices.

Coco-Loco Cake

As this recipe demonstrates, you can have your Paleo and eat cake, too. This makes a wonderful birthday treat. The cinnamon adds an extra "something," but it's optional.

Makes 6 to 8 servings.

1 cup almond flour

3 tablespoons unsweetened cocoa powder

1 teaspoon cinnamon (optional)

2 teaspoon baking powder

½ cup coconut crystals (or honey)

¾ cup melted coconut oil

1 tablespoon 100% vanilla extract

¾ cup coconut milk

3 large eggs

¼ cup dark chocolate chips

1. Take a large piece of parchment paper and fit it into the slow cooker to line the bottom and sides, allowing for some of the paper to come over the lip. This will help you remove the cake when it's cooked.

2. In a bowl, combine the almond flour, cocoa powder, cinnamon, baking powder, and coconut crystals. Set aside.

3. In a separate bowl, combine the coconut oil with the vanilla, then add the coconut milk and stir to combine well. Add the eggs one by one, stirring well after each addition.

4. Fold the dry mixture into the wet mixture until combined thoroughly. Stir in the chocolate chips.

5. Transfer the cake to the slow cooker. Cover and cut away any excess parchment paper and ensure the lid is fitting properly. Cook on Low for 2 to 3 hours until cake is firm but not dry.

6. Lift the cake out using the parchment paper, and flip onto a serving plate. Allow to cool.

While it's doubtful our Paleolithic ancestors ate chocolate as we know it, as part of our modern society, it's hard to resist entirely. There's a great discussion of the pros and cons of chocolate—and coffee—on the website paleodietlifestyle.com, which basically argues that dark chocolate is a suitable Paleo treat, not to be eaten in excess, but to be enjoyed on occasion.

Baked Peaches

Ripe peaches are so juicy that, when slow-cooked, they make a summer slurry. Stir in some toasted nuts for added crunch when serving.

Makes 4 servings.

4 large, ripe peaches, peeled, pits removed, and cut into chunks or slices

1 teaspoon cinnamon

1 teaspoon lemon zest

2 tablespoons honey

1. Put the peach slices into the slow cooker. Sprinkle with cinnamon and lemon zest. Drizzle with honey.

2. Cover and cook on Low for 3 to 4 hours or on High for about 2 hours. Serve warm or at room temperature.

Variation:

* Turn the recipe into a crumble or crisp by adding a topping of ½ cup almond flour mixed with 1 tablespoon coconut butter and some toasted almonds. Put the crumble on top of the fruit before cooking.

Chocolate Mousse

The name of this dessert is ironic considering it's for a Paleo diet. It's not the "moose" our Paleo ancestors were savoring, that's for sure. But it's one for our modern world.

Makes 6 to 8 servings.

5 egg yolks

2 cups coconut milk

½ cup coconut crystals

1 teaspoon vanilla extract

¼ cup unsweetened cocoa powder

1. Put an oven-safe casserole dish in the slow cooker. Add water around the dish so that it reaches about halfway up the side of the dish.

2. In a large bowl using a whisk, beat the egg yolks until thoroughly combined and a lighter, lemony color. Add the coconut milk, crystals, vanilla, and cocoa powder until well combined. Pour the mixture into the dish inside the slow cooker.

3. Cover and cook on Low for 5 to 6 hours or on High for 2 to 4 hours. The mousse should be thick but not too firm. Turn the cooker off and let the dish cool slightly in the water. Then remove it and refrigerate for an hour or longer before serving.

Top this dish with fresh raspberries for a really elegant and decadent dessert.

Pumpkin Custard

You can use canned organic pumpkin puree for this recipe, or you can use freshly baked or steamed pumpkin.

Makes 6 to 8 servings.

6 egg yolks

1¼ cups coconut milk

1 teaspoon pumpkin pie spice mix

½ cup coconut crystals

½ teaspoon vanilla extract

⅛ teaspoon salt

⅓ cup pumpkin puree

1. Put an oven-safe casserole dish in the slow cooker. Add water around the dish so that it reaches about halfway up the side of the dish.

2. In a large bowl using a whisk, beat the egg yolks until thoroughly combined and a lighter, lemony color. Add the coconut milk, spice mix, crystals, vanilla, and salt until well combined. Fold in the pumpkin puree. Pour the mixture into the dish inside the slow cooker.

3. Cover and cook on Low for 5 to 6 hours or on High for 2 to 4 hours. The custard should be thick but not too firm. Turn the cooker off and let the dish cool slightly in the water. Then remove it and refrigerate for an hour or longer before serving.

Pumpkin pie spice mix is a pre-made combination of cinnamon, ginger, nutmeg, and allspice. If you'd like to experiment with bringing out certain of these flavors, use them individually.

Honey-Kissed Fig

This makes a Fig Newton–like substance that has all the freshness of the figs without the additives found in the highly processed cookie centers.

Makes about 2 cups.

2 lbs fresh figs, stems removed, peeled and cut into eighths

Juice from 1 lemon

½ cup water

½ cup honey

1. Put the peeled and cut figs in the slow cooker. Squeeze the lemon over the fruit, removing the seeds that come out. Combine the water and honey in a bowl and mix. Pour over the figs.

2. Cover and cook on Low 6 to 8 hours or on High for 4 to 5 hours. Allow to cool before serving.

Figs are actually one of the oldest known fruits, originating in northern Asia Minor—so it might have been the true treat of our Paleo ancestors. They were cooked to use as sweeteners long before the discovery of sugar. Figs are loaded with fiber, iron, and potassium.

Paleo-Friendly Foods, A to Z

This list isn't all-inclusive, but it's a handy quick reference when you want to whip something together and you're just not sure if your ingredients are Paleo-approved. For unusual ingredients that might not be on the list, research them online. It's a great way to get involved in Paleo discussions.

Adobe Sauce
Allspice
Almonds—nuts, butter, flour, milk
Apples—all types
Apple Butter
Apple Cider Vinegar
Arrowroot Powder
Artichokes
Avocado—fruit and oil
Bacon
Baking Soda
Balsamic Vinegar
Bananas
Basil
Bay Leaf
Beef—broth/stock, whole, parts (as fresh as possible)
Beets
Blackberries
Black Pepper
Blueberries
Broccoli
Brussels Sprouts
Cabbage—all types
Capers
Carrots
Cashews—nuts and butter
Cauliflower
Cayenne Pepper
Celery
Cherries

Chicken—broth/stock, whole, parts (as fresh as possible)
Chilis—all types
Chili Powder
Chipotle
Chocolate (dark)
Chocolate Chips (dark)
Chorizo (as fresh as possible)
Cilantro—fresh and dried
Cinnamon—sticks and ground
Clementine
Cloves—whole and ground
Cocoa Powder, unsweetened
Coconut—fruit, aminos, butter, cream, flakes, flour, milk, oil (unsweetened)
Coffee
Coriander—seeds and ground
Cucumber
Cumin
Curry Powder
Dates
Dijon Mustard
Eggs—yolks and whites
Figs
Fish—all
Fish Sauce
Flaxseed—oil, meal, flour
Fruit—all
Garlic—cloves, powder, dried
Ginger—root, powder, fresh and dried
Grapes
Green Chilis
Green Onions
Green Pepper
Herbes de Provence
Honey
Hot Sauce
Italian Sausage
Italian Seasoning
Jalapenos
Kale

Lamb—chops, ribs, leg, roast, shoulder (all), fresh

Lemon—all parts, fresh

Lime—all parts, fresh

Macadamia—nuts, butter

Mango

Maple Syrup

Mushrooms—button, domestic, Portobello, crimini, shiitake, all types (fresh)

Mustard—powder, seeds

Nut Butters—all except peanut butter

Nutmeg—fresh and dried

Olive Oil

Olives—all types

Onion—yellow, white, red, pearl (all types)—fresh or frozen, unprocessed

Orange—all parts, fresh

Oregano—fresh and dried

Paprika—sweet and hot

Parsley—fresh and dried

Peach

Pecans—raw, butter

Pickles

Pineapple

Pistachios

Plantains

Poblano Pepper

Poppy Seeds

Pork—chops, ribs, bacon, sausage, offal (as fresh as possible)

Portobello Mushrooms

Protein Powder

Pumpkin—vegetable, seeds (unprocessed)

Raisins

Red Onion

Red Pepper

Red Pepper Flakes

Red Wine

Red Wine Vinegar

Rosemary—fresh and dried

Sage—fresh and dried

Salmon

Scallions

Sesame Oil

Shallots

Short Ribs

Shrimp—raw, cooked, frozen (unprocessed)

Spinach

Squash

Strawberries

Sun-dried Tomatoes

Sweet Potatoes

Tilapia

Tomato—fruit, and unseasoned canned, diced, sauce, paste

Turkey—whole, ground, pieces (unprocessed)

Unsweetened Cacao Powder

Unsweetened Coconut Flakes

Unsweetened Coconut Powder

Unsweetened Shredded Coconut

Vegetable Broth

Vegetables—all except legumes

Walnut—nuts, oil, and butter

White Wine Vinegar

Yellow Mustard

Zucchini

Vanilla—bean, extract

Index

About Cider Mill Press
Book Publishers

Good ideas ripen with time. From seed to harvest, Cider Mill Press brings fine reading, information, and entertainment together between the covers of its creatively crafted books. Our Cider Mill bears fruit twice a year, publishing a new crop of titles each spring and fall.

Visit us on the Web at
www.cidermillpress.com
or write to us at
12 Spring Street
PO Box 454
Kennebunkport, Maine 04046